Head of the Class

Head of the Class:

A Teen Dog Expert Teaches You to Raise and Train the Perfect Pal

Kate Eldredge with
Debra M. Eldredge, DVM

Howell
Book House™

This book is printed on acid-free paper. ♾

Howell Book House
Published by Wiley Publishing, Inc., Hoboken, New Jersey

For general information on our other products and services or to obtain technical support please contact our Customer Care Department within the U.S. at (800) 762-2974, outside the U.S. at (317) 572-3993 or fax (317) 572-4002.

Wiley also publishes its books in a variety of electronic formats. Some content that appears in print may not be available in electronic books. For more information about Wiley products, please visit our web site at www.wiley.com.

Library of Congress Cataloging-in-Publication Data: Is Available from Publisher

ISBN 13 978-0-471-77962-9

ISBN 10 0-471-77962-8

Printed in the United States of America

10 9 8 7 6 5 4 3 2 1

Book design by Erin Zeltner
Cover design by Wendy Mount
Book production by Wiley Publishing, Inc. Composition Services

Dedication

We would like to dedicate this book to the many wonderful family dogs who have left us and wait at the Rainbow Bridge for us: the large but gentle German Shepherd dog Cyrus; the silly Belgian Tervuren Wiley; Gus, the amazing Labrador Retriever from a shelter; Bubba, the huge but sweet Kuvasz; and Beep, the heart dog of Deb's life. We would also like to dedicate this book to the beloved family dogs whom many of you have known and the ones waiting for you in the future.

Table of Contents

Preface

This book is intended as a guide to help you and your family enjoy one of the best companions imaginable—a great dog! We have teamed up to help you add a dog to your family and make it a decision you will never regret. I'm Kate Eldredge, a kid and a dog owner and trainer. I have enjoyed all of our family dogs all my life, and now I have three dogs of my own. My co-author is Deb M. Eldredge, DVM, my mother and a dog owner as well as a veterinarian. Deb has had dogs for many years: one of her own when she was a child, family dogs as an adult, and her own personal dogs to train. Together, we start by helping you decide whether a dog is right for you, and then which dog to choose and how to prepare for your new family member. This is one of those rare cases where you actually get to choose a family member! We hope to get you off on the right foot, or right paw as it may be, with information on basic care and training.

After you and your dog have the basics down, there is a wonderful world of dog sports and activities awaiting you. We hope that you will be inspired to try some of these dog activities, and we provide guidance and resources to help you along the way. These activities can be done for competition or simply for fun and enjoyment.

Several chapters are dedicated to caring for your dog along with some health information and tips for going places with your dog. We also included some craft and cooking ideas that can be lots of fun on a rainy day. Each chapter also has a section just for parents that includes tips, guidelines, and a few rules.

Dogs really are man's best friend, and we hope that this book will make your relationship with your dog one of the best in your life.

We recently added a new family member, Queezle, a Belgian Tervuren puppy. She is technically my dog, so I am responsible for training and care. Queezle learns very fast and has picked up several habits from our other dogs, including jumping up on the back door when she wants to come inside. Teaching Come was very easy, since she loves treats and praise. Down was a little harder; she has so much energy that often she will launch herself into the air from a Down. She is by far our sweetest dog and very clever. She is benefiting from all that we have learned with our other dogs.

It can be tricky to find time to spend with each dog when you have many dogs, as they all want lots of attention, but we make sure to spend some special private time with each one every day. If nothing else, they get to take turns driving to band practice.

By having dogs, I have had the chance to travel, have learned poise, and have gained confidence and been able to achieve many goals in 4-H and open dog showing. I have learned that if you work hard, you can achieve success, but you must use patience, persistence, and kindness at all times. Deb has had wonderful assistants to teach her kids patience, responsibility, and how to scoop poop. Plus, dogs are cheaper than a nanny.

We hope our book will help you to integrate a dog (or two or three) into your family and to enjoy their companionship to the fullest.

Acknowledgments

Many thanks to our photographers—Tom Eldredge, Heather Gould, and Linda Aloi in particular—who contributed multiple photos, and to Linda's son Chris Aloi, who ended up being a technical consultant. Thanks to our agent, Jessica Faust, home with her new baby boy, Sawyer, and to Pam Mourouzis, who believed in this book. Thanks to Tere Stouffer, our development editor, who probably has a few new gray hairs courtesy of us. And special thanks to our kid/dog profile teams: Tom and Baloo, Holly and Soda Pop, Margo and Raisin, Jamie and Buddy, Brie and Blaze, Amanda and Spencer, Matt and BooBoo, Katelyn and Jake, Sarah and Sooner, Cecelia and Sage, Becky and Robbie, and Kate's dogs Flash and Queezle. A special thanks to Betsy Atkinson for letting us share Hunter's story.

Extra thanks to Dani, Hokey, and Susan, who helped Deb and Kate stay on task, and Tia, who was a bit put out that she is only featured in photos, not in a profile. Special thanks to Chuck, who put up with a messy study and various computer crises. Also thanks to Dani, Hokey, Queezle, Susan, Flash, Baloo, and Tia, who modeled for several photos and tried out a few of the dog cookie recipes.

Foreword

A few years ago, my partner on the telecast of the Westminster Kennel Club's Annual Dog Show on USA Network was chuckling about the look in a particular dog's eye as it was on camera.

"I wonder what he's thinking," he asked me. "Don't you wish they could talk?"

I had a quick answer: "Oh, no . . . they wouldn't be nearly as much fun if they could."

I really do believe that, but I know what they would say anyway: "Me too, me too!"

My dogs always want to be with me, whether it's at home, on their same old walk around the neighborhood, or on an adventure somewhere new. They're smiling and laughing with their eyes and their tails, everyone is their friend, and they're never quite ready to go home—unless, of course, it's D-I-N-N-E-R time.

And I love that about them. I also love the fact that they listen to me and that I know I can count on them to treat everything I say to them as profound, entertaining, and funny.

The fact is that today we have an emotional and spiritual connection to our dogs. We treat them as members of the family and include them in nearly everything we do. We plan our daily schedules and vacations around them and with them.

And the Eldredges took all of these principles and created a veritable guide for you and your ultimate companion (you may have to read it out loud for your dog). The lessons begin with finding the right dog for your lifestyle and properly preparing your family for the lifelong and life-altering experience.

Other lessons in this book include responsible dog ownership, making the journey with your dog fun and productive for everyone involved, and taking care of your dog as you share your life and your activities.

Along the way, you will find that, quite simply, dogs are good for you. They are good for your mental health and good for your physical health. In fact, according to the Delta Society, the world's leading advocate for therapy animals, children raised with pets learn compassion, develop self-esteem and self-confidence, expand communication skills, develop responsibility, and mature in their respect for other living things.

And for adults and children alike, animals provide a therapeutic touch. Just petting a dog can lower one's blood pressure, and living with a dog does the same. A study at the University of Missouri–Columbia Center for the Study of Animal Wellness showed that when a human pets a dog, almost immediately a large amount of hormones are activated that are associated with health and feelings of well-being. Pets also keep people moving, physically and socially: Seniors who have pets have far fewer doctor visits than those who don't.

Puppies, dogs, children, and adults—having a dog in the family is good for everyone. This book helps you create and enjoy that relationship and helps you understand your dog a little better.

And as you apply what you read in this book, sharing your life with your dog and teaching your dog how to be a responsible member of the family and the community, remember this: What you teach your dog is not as important as what you learn from your dog.

David Frei

David Frei is the voice of the Westminster Kennel Club on USA Network and of the National Dog Show on NBC.

Are You Ready for Parenthood?

When you acquire your very own dog or puppy, it is like having a baby in the house. Only *you* are now the parent! The family dog may have been your sibling, but with your own dog, you are now the person of authority and the person responsible for someone else. Pet ownership means that you may sometimes have to give up your own fun activities in order to care for your dog properly—just like your parents need to sacrifice for you sometimes. Still, having a dog has so many rewards of its own that you will probably not even notice.

Why Dogs Are Good for Kids

Dogs are good for you for many reasons. A dog is a friend who will always be there for you, 24/7. Your dog is never too busy to hang out with you and is always willing to try anything you want—be it a midnight snack or an early morning jog in the park. A dog will sleep in with you or get up early with no complaints.

A dog provides unconditional love, even when you are having a bad day or are in a bad mood. A dog won't care if your hair is a mess, you flunked your math test, or you were dead last in the cross-country meet. Your dog won't even care if you snore at night; he probably snores too!

Kids and dogs keep each other in great shape.

For those who are competitive, your dog is a dear partner, not a rival. Together, you may be a competitive team, but you never compete against each other. Your dog will try to cover for you—even take the blame for missing homework. As seen in the photo, dogs help you to get exercise while they are exercising, too.

Your dog is a great sounding board. You can practice your public speaking without fear of hysterical laughter or cruel criticism. You can tell your dog all your secrets with no fear of discovery. He will support you when you complain about your unjust parents and rejoice with you when you ace your science project. He may even help out with your science fair project by being a willing subject for checking heart rates or learning operant conditioning with a clicker, just like Pavlov's dogs drooling for dinner when they heard the dinner bell.

Your dog will also be your guardian angel. He will alert you to any dangers and drive off intruders with a bark or a growl. He will accompany you when you jog and discourage any unwanted attention. Your dog doesn't need power like a security system does; he is always working for you, and the price is right!

A dog of your very own will teach you about responsibility, compassion, empathy, sorrow, and happiness, and enjoying every minute of every day and every bit of mud.

Baloo can handle anything—even posing as a surfer dude!

Why Kids Are Good for Dogs

Kids are some of the best puppy and dog socializers in the world. Kids naturally assume that a dog will handle almost anything, and their confidence gives the dog confidence. A dog who grows up with kids is exposed to all kinds of things, from loud toys and interesting music to crazy outfits. Check out our surfer Aussie in the photo. Kids give a dog a chance to learn that people who move quickly or erratically or who scream and make crazy noises are just versions of a normal human. A dog with kid experience learns that people come in all sizes, shapes, and volume levels.

Dogs and kids both benefit from their relationship in terms of exercise. Your dog will need daily exercise and walks, which means you get daily exercise and walks, too. Kids tend to be more active than many adults, so they will be happy to take the dog for long walks, throw the ball for an hour, or play tug-of-war. Dogs are often seen at kid sports events—either as loyal fans or devoted mascots. Running laps with the soccer team is good exercise for your dog.

A dog who has grown up with kids will have learned all about silly games. He will know about being a good bed buddy and not hogging the covers. He will tolerate wearing T-shirts or funky hats and may even have learned to rush to the chairs while playing musical chairs. He will know not to bite the kids on the sleds as they fly down the hill or to tear at clothing on bike riders.

A dog should be allowed to sleep on the bed only if he respects the person in the bed—not growling if you roll over, always getting off when told to, and never threatening your authority. A well-behaved dog can keep you nice and warm on a cold night.

Kids often have more free time than most adults and willingly spend plenty of it with the dog. They can play with the dog right after school before settling down to do homework. On weekends, they are often free to exercise and train the dog. The extra attention is great for the dog, and as noted, is good for the kid, too.

Responsible Dog Ownership

Adding a dog to your family means added responsibilities to your community as well. You want your dog to be a welcome addition to the neighborhood, not a source of irritation. There are many ways to accomplish this.

A leash with a responsible person on the other end is one of the most important items in your dog's life. While on leash and with you, your dog can't chase the neighbor's cat, dig up a prized flowerbed, or chase a car and be injured or cause an accident. Whenever your dog leaves your property, he should be on a leash.

It is *extremely* important that all families clean up after their dogs. Leaving dog waste around for people to step in, causing bad odors or even leading to health problems, is not being responsible. Get a pooper scooper for your walks or carry poop bags. Along with cleaning up poop, don't let your dog urinate on people's flowers, trash cans, or cars.

Picking up poop sounds awful, but it is a skill you can quickly acquire. Some people prefer a scoop to snag their dog's poop and then carry it home or to a lined trash can. The most common method, however, is to use a baggie. You can practice at home picking up a dog biscuit. Put a biscuit on the floor. Then slip a baggie over your hand. Carefully reach down and pick up the biscuit. Then turn the bag inside out over the biscuit. Voilà! A twist tie helps to keep the odor down until you reach a trash can.

Picking up your dog's poop and keeping him on leash are very important steps in being a good dog neighbor. It is also important to keep your dog from barking—especially late at night or early in the morning. Most dogs bark from loneliness and boredom, so keep your dog inside or with you.

There are laws regarding dogs in many communities. Rabies vaccinations are required in the United States for public health reasons. Most communities require a license for dogs, and many have leash laws that limit when and where a dog may run while off leash. Respecting these laws is an important part of responsible dog ownership.

It is also important to make sure that your dog does not get involved in producing unplanned puppies. Spaying and neutering help control pet overpopulation and also keep the number of dogs euthanized for lack of good homes down. A spayed or neutered dog also has no chance of testicular or uterine cancer and reduced chances of mammary and breast cancers. Many behavior problems can be reduced or even eliminated with spaying and neutering.

A well-behaved dog is a ticket to opportunities in your community—doing therapy dog visits to nursing homes, working with children in schools, or being allowed to attend sports functions. Make sure *your* dog is a great canine ambassador.

The Right Dog for You

Not every dog is right for every person. You need to do your homework so that you end up with just the right companion for you.

One of the first major decisions to make is whether you want a puppy or an adult dog. A puppy will require a much bigger time commitment initially. Puppies need frequent bathroom breaks, extra meals, lots of naps, and lots of patience. A puppy is more likely than a dog to chew your dearest possessions or dig a large hole in your mother's flower garden. A puppy is, of course, very cute and will grow up with you. Remember that puppies do grow; this pair of Belgian Tervurens shows the difference in size in a puppy and adult of that breed. Your puppy's personality will be partly shaped by your efforts and training. Drawbacks include the fact that you can't be sure of your puppy's adult temperament or his physical soundness. With a mixed breed puppy, you may just have to guess at his adult size and type of coat.

Puppy or dog? The choice can be a difficult one.

An adult dog won't be quite as cute as a puppy, but with any luck, the adult dog you choose will be housetrained, will be past the worst of the chewing stage, and might even have some basic training. You will know his size, type of coat, and basic temperament. An adult dog can bond just as strongly to you as a puppy, and many adult dogs who have had rough lives seem grateful to have a loving human of their very own. Your adult dog may come with some baggage from previous homes, such as bad habits that you will need to retrain.

You need to consider many factors when you think of your ideal companion. (Your parents may want to offer some input here, too.) You should check out some good books about dog breeds and look at the behavior of groups of dogs as well as what they look like. Scenthounds and sighthounds vary greatly in the way they look at life, for example. Attending a dog show and checking out the various breeds, as well as talking to competitors, may help you decide which dog is best for you.

Financial considerations can be important, too—basically, who is paying for the dog and his expenses? Some dogs require professional grooming, which is an additional expense, but others require minimal efforts to stay clean. Grooming is expensive; who is paying, you or your parents? A large dog will need more dog food and bigger, more expensive beds and toys.

An active dog needs a definite commitment for daily exercise—even if it is raining or snowing. Even a couch potato needs daily walks. Some breeds are easier to train than others. For example, herding breeds tend to be easier to train than hounds. If you are already planning to compete in any dog sports, you need to take that into consideration. Still, the bottom line will be what breed or dog makes your heart flutter, lights up your eyes, and calls out, "Take *me* home!"

Where do you find your canine companion? The answer can vary with what you want. Adorable and talented mixed breeds may be available as puppies or adults at your local Humane Society or shelter. Look for a healthy partner and, if possible, one who has had some behavior screening by trained shelter personnel. Avoid pet stores, as many of the puppies come from puppy mills and may not have had good early socialization. Plus, their housetraining may be tough because they are used to living in a cage where they also eliminate.

A purebred dog may be found in a shelter, via a rescue group, or from a reputable breeder. Avoid the breeder who keeps the dogs out in the garage or a shed and who can't tell you about health clearances. Rescue groups usually screen their dogs for health problems and temperament. Reputable breeders screen their dogs for health problems and do their best to give their puppies an excellent start in life with good nutrition, clean living

Choosing the Perfect Dog for You

Keep the following factors in mind when choosing the perfect dog for you:

- **Coat type:** Remember that *you* will be doing the grooming and vacuuming the hair (professional grooming is expensive).
- **Size:** If you have size 10 feet, a Chihuahua may not be the best choice, but large dogs cost more to feed and care for.
- **Exercise:** How much do you like to run or walk? Some dogs require several hours of exercise every day.
- **Ease of training:** Herding and sporting breeds are generally the easiest to train.
- **Temperament:** If you expect your dog to be a watchdog, avoid a party puppy.

quarters, and plenty of socialization. Don't rule out a breeder if you want an adult dog. A breeder may have a wonderful adult dog who is retired from the show ring or just not suitable for breeding and who would love to have a kid of his own.

Reputable breeders will do temperament testing to try to match each puppy with the best possible home. Such a breeder will ask *you* just as many questions as you ask them—maybe even more!

The Human-Animal Bond

The relationship between a kid and her very own dog is a very special one. It is a relationship of mutual trust and love unmatched by any other. Your dog looks to you as the light of his life, while you can confide anything in your dog, knowing that your secrets are safe and that he will listen to all your problems. Your dog never judges you and always stands by you—unless you make a mistake on the agility course!

Respect should be an important part of the bond between you and your dog. Even though you will always be partners, you should still be the authority figure, much like a team captain or a parent. As a pack animal, your dog is happiest with a leader—but that leader must be kind and fair. Just as your parents set limits for you, you need to set limits and guidelines for your dog.

For Parents Only

Dear parents: Your first grandchild has a furry face! This is your chance to learn how to be a good grandparent. You will need to offer advice without overpowering your child. You need to let your child assume the primary responsibility for taking care of the dog, but since we are talking about a living being, you do need to check in now and then.

As the adult, you will probably have to deal with emergencies and may be counted on for financial help. Your child may need help with training or even basic care—for example, if she has a band trip and you are left with the dog.

Also, be aware that most dogs live for 10 or more years. It is highly likely that you will be responsible for your child's dog for at least a year or two when she heads out into the world to college or her first job. Think of dog ownership as an excellent way to handle your empty nest syndrome.

The big plus here is that you get to spoil and play with the dog, just like any regular grandparent. And if the puppy has an accident, you can call on your child to clean it up!

Profile: Tom with Susan and Baloo

Tom is a kid who has had both an adult dog and a puppy of his own. Susan is a Pembroke Welsh Corgi who needed a new home when her breeder went through a divorce and had to sell her home and place many of her dogs. At the time, Susan was 8 years old and a very well-trained dog. Tom was 7 years old and ready for the responsibilities of a dog of his own, especially with the lesser commitment needed for an adult dog.

Susan fit right in, and Tom didn't have to go through the hassles of housetraining or puppy chewing. Tom sang silly songs to Susan, let her sleep on his bed, and called her his "Poochy-coo." Since Susan was already trained, Tom could go right out and compete with her. They even took Reserve Grand Champion in Open Agility at the New York State Fair.

Still, Susan had been an adult's dog, and after about two years, she decided that she basically wanted to retire and be Tom's mother's dog.

Tom and Baloo are best buddies and soul mates.

So it was time to find just the right puppy for Tom. He wanted an Australian Shepherd, and there are many good Aussie breeders in our area. Tom found a litter whose sire was owned and trained by a 13-year-old kid. He knew the sire and the grandsire, and they were excellent kid dogs. Tom used a unique method to select his exact puppy. He had his choice down to two of the lovely puppies in the litter—all healthy, and all nice according to their puppy testing. He had the two puppies held at one end of the field, and he went to the other end and called "Puppy, puppy!" One pup stood up and piddled, while the other pup tore across the grass into Tom's arms.

Tom was 9 years old then and ready for the added responsibility of raising a puppy. Baloo came home in May, so Tom did need help with housetraining until school was out. Still, Tom did all of Baloo's chores like feeding, training, and grooming, plus most of his walks and exercising.

Tom feels it is great to have a dog of his own. He doesn't have to share him; Baloo sleeps on the end of his bed—keeping his feet warm—and Baloo is totally devoted to Tom. As you can see in the photo, Tom and Baloo are best buds. Tom says Baloo is special because he has mixed eyes (one blue, one brown) and a wiggly butt, and is always willing to play—even if it is just catching snowballs. Baloo makes Tom feel happy and even cheers him up if he is sad. The biggest drawback for Tom of having a dog of his own is having to walk Baloo even if it's rainy or cold and snowy outside.

Tom and Baloo train and compete in every dog sport they can, from flyball to agility to herding and even skijoring! They have done very well in prenovice obedience and in junior showmanship—even taking Reserve Grand Champion in Grooming and Handling B at the New York State Fair.

"Baloo is my very best friend," says Tom. "He has taught me patience and to try and be calm even in very frustrating situations." In his case, Tom feels a puppy was the right dog for him when he was old enough for the responsibility. He feels that Baloo formed an even stronger bond with him than Susan and that an active, crazy dog is the very best match for him now.

2

Preschool and Kindergarten: Getting Ready for Dog Ownership

Just as with a human baby, you need to prepare for your new puppy (or dog). A puppy shower would be fun, but you need to think about the essentials for your puppy, too. Getting your home and your whole family ready for a new member is just like getting a child ready to head off and start school. Remember those lunch boxes and alphabet cards? This time, think leash, collar, and treats. And just as safety is important in school, it is very important at home. Plus everyone needs to agree on policies and rules for making your puppy a beloved member of your family.

Puppy/Dog-Proofing Your Home

Just as your parents baby-proofed the house for you, now *you* need to accident-proof the house for your baby—a baby with four legs. Baby gates are almost essential for managing a new canine member of the family. A gate can keep your pup out of the living room where your mother has her collection of delicate china or away from your dad's workshop with tools and dangerous chemicals. You can also use baby gates to confine your

Recommended Equipment

Just as people often have baby showers for new human family members, sometimes friends will arrange a puppy shower. If so, these are items you will need. Otherwise, have fun shopping yourself.

- **Collar:** Go for safe, not just cute. Slip collars are not safe to be left on dogs. Remember that your puppy will grow, so you need to check her collar frequently.
- **Leash:** You want a leash that is comfortable for *your* hand. Leather is the most comfortable, but some nylon leads work well, too.
- **Bowls:** Ceramic or stainless steel are long lasting, easy to clean, and nonallergenic. You will need at least two bowls: one for food and one for water.
- **Crate:** Think of the crate as your puppy's personal bedroom. It is a place of safety and quiet, a place of rest. You may want more than one: one for the car if you travel with your dog, one for your bedroom, and one in a busy area of the house so that your pup can be safely out of the way but still in the thick of things.
- **Bed:** This can be a deluxe sheepskin cedar chip pillow or a simple old comforter. Remember to keep it clean.
- **Food and treats:** You should discuss the ideal food for your pup with her breeder and your veterinarian. They can guide you to just the right diet to help your pup grow properly. Check on treats as well—you will want treats for training, and it is important that the treats are healthy, too.
- **Toys:** Toys are important as well as fun. Toys can be used for training, exercising, and bonding. Make sure that the toys are appropriate for your dog—a small dog may have trouble carrying a tennis ball. Beware of toys that can be chewed. Never leave your dog alone with a potentially hazardous toy.
- **Identification:** You want to be sure that if your dog gets loose, she will be returned to you. A collar with tags, a microchip, or a tattoo are all possible means of identification.

puppy to the room you are working in (doing homework, for example) so that she is under your watchful eye. Plus the whole family gets limber learning to step over the gates!

Dogs are scenting machines, so the smells of trash, garbage, and many toxins may entice them. You will need lids on your garbage cans, although

Who is to blame, the cute puppy or the child who wasn't watching her?

some dogs even learn to open these. If you have a brilliant dog, you may need to raise the cans up or even shut them in a closet. Medicines and cleaning supplies need to be kept in raised or locked cupboards. The locks that work for babies work great for puppies, too. Don't forget the dangerous materials out in the garage or down in the basement; your dog shouldn't go in those areas unsupervised.

Look at your house from your puppy's point of view. Things that look fun to play with or chew include electrical cords, books, shoes, and human toys. You may not have thought of toilet paper as a toy, but the puppy in our photos certainly did! Electrical cords need to be moved safely next to walls and can be covered with carpet or hose material. Cords tend to get chewed when they are blocking your pup's path and she figures it is easier to chew through than go under or around. Puppies love things with your scent on them, and your sneakers are, therefore, *very* attractive. Don't leave anything you are attached to or don't want destroyed or marked with cute little tooth marks where your puppy can get it.

Other pets you have as family members may not be as thrilled with your new addition as you are. Older dogs will need a safe place where they can escape from the "monster" and get some well-deserved rest. The same goes for cats and house bunnies. This is another good use for baby gates. A large dog can jump over the baby gate that confines the pup. If your pup is large, leaving a space at the bottom allows your cat or bunny to zip under, leaving a disappointed pup on the other side.

A baby gate can also be used to block off a room where your other pets have their food dishes and litter boxes. If you have birds, be aware that a puppy might try to jump up at the cage or go after a parrot that is used to having free run of the house. You hope that everyone eventually will learn to accept or at least tolerate the new family member.

Your yard is another area that needs to be puppy-proofed. Poisonous plants need to be removed or closed off from your curious pup, who might want to chew on them. Fencing that has securely held your large Labrador Retriever may not keep a Shih Tzu pup safely confined. Walk your fence line and look for holes—either in the fence or under it. Check gates as well, as they may have larger spaces where a pup could slip through. Some puppies are expert climbers, so check for things a pup could use to get up on and then go over the fence. Swimming pools should have puppy-proof fencing around them to prevent drownings.

Establishing House Rules

It is very important that your family sit down and decide what rules will apply to your new family member. Furniture is often one of the first areas of controversy. If your mom has a beautiful white sofa, she will probably not want your dog lying on it. On the other hand, perhaps the couch in the family room could be made "dog acceptable" with the addition of a washable cover. Many families choose one chair to be their dog's, or they add a dog bed or blanket to the family room so that their dog can join them while they watch TV, read, or play games.

Dogs do not *need* to be on the furniture, and if your family will be happier with the dog on the floor, just establish that rule right from the start. If your pup is never allowed on the sofa, she won't miss it. On the other hand, if you adopt an older dog who has been allowed to sleep on chairs, it might take a while for her to learn that this is no longer allowed. Be patient, but consistent. And remember our earlier discussion of bed rules: *no* sleeping on the bed if your dog growls or acts possessive of the bed.

Kitchen and dining room behavior is usually the second biggest area of rule discussions. Many families like having their dogs around while they eat, but no one likes a dog head resting on the table staring hopefully at their plate, drool dripping on their knees, or feeling they need to guard their food at all times. Plus, your mom shouldn't have to worry about leaving food on the counter as she prepares dinner.

You can place a blanket or a bed in the kitchen and teach your dog to lie on it quietly or just to lie near the table. You might also decide simply to have your dog stay out of the kitchen during meals and rest in a nearby room or a doorway. Again, be consistent; letting your dog hang out in the kitchen for breakfast on weekends but expecting her to quietly lie in a nearby room on weekdays just won't work.

Dining Rules

Even small dogs can steal food. Kate's Corgi, Flash, uses chairs and will happily set herself up on tables. Keep chairs pushed in by the table and don't leave tasty snacks on a low coffee table. *Never* feed your dog tidbits from the table.

Waiting in doorways is a safety issue as well as good manners.

One area where every dog should respect some rules is doorways. A dog who rushes out of doors is a danger to herself and anyone nearby. If she runs out of the house, she could get hit by a car or take off after a jogger. In her headlong dash to be first out the door, she might knock over Grandma and cause her to break her hip. It is much better to teach your dog a Back command at doors and/or to make her wait each time you open a door until you tell her it is OK to go through. Surprisingly, dogs learn rules about spaces and places very quickly. The dogs pictured here all wait at an open door.

How to greet people is a skill that all dogs should learn. Once again, your family needs to decide what is acceptable and then all follow through consistently. Small dogs often get away with jumping up on people, but even small dogs may get mud on clothes, tear stockings, and so on. Certainly a big dog jumping up on someone could frighten or injure them.

It is best if your dog learns to sit to greet people and be gently petted on the head. You can still teach your dog to leap up on *you* on command if you like a flying greeting for yourself. Just remember, your dog may be excited and give you that flying greeting when you are wearing your best outfit and she has wet, muddy paws. As you can see in the photos on page 16, these two greetings draw very different reactions.

Housetraining is an essential skill for all pet dogs. Although you are to be the main caretaker for your puppy—think of yourself as a nanny, or, if you are a boy, as Arnold Schwarzenegger in *Kindergarten Cop*—other family members will probably have to help during the first months of housetraining.

Once again, make sure that everybody is on the same page. No hitting the puppy for an accident. Simply put the puppy outside while you clean up the mess and perhaps whack yourself on the head with a newspaper—a clean, dry one—for forgetting to keep a close eye on your pup. We have found it works best to start out with a "bathroom word" right away. When our dogs go out in the yard and we say "Hurry go pee" or "Hurry go poop," they have learned that this means they will be left for a while or will be riding in the car, so they need to empty out right away. Just make sure that everyone uses the same words.

The dog who sits quietly to greet people is a welcome guest, but a dog who jumps on people can be a menace.

Who's in Charge, or Who's on First?

Even if this is *your* very own, beloved dog, you still need to establish who will be in charge of what. And very often, like it or not, you will have to share your dog with other family members. Just keep in mind that that means sharing the work, too.

With a puppy or older dog who is not well housetrained, you need a plan for who will be taking the dog out late at night and who will take her out first thing in the morning. Often, parents will be up first and stay up latest, and they may be willing to take the puppy out at those times. Still, if your little darling wakes up and cries at 3 A.M., *you* should be the one taking her out.

Along with the important walks for going to the bathroom, your dog will need to have someone in charge of her food and water. It is a good idea to have one person in charge of this, although others can help. This way your pup won't miss a meal, but she won't get extra meals either. It also means there will be someone who knows just how much your pup needs to be fed and who keeps track of how well and how much she eats. And don't forget to let your parents know if the dog food is getting low. Check the water bowls frequently and put fresh water in at least twice a day. Who wants warm, stale water?

Rules for Rules

- **Be consistent:** That means the whole family has to agree and follow through on any decisions, plus use the same commands.
- **Be fair:** Don't expect your dog to differentiate between a new sofa and an old one (for example).
- **Be firm:** Don't give in because it is your dog's birthday—if she gets to sleep on the bed just once, she will try to do it again.
- **Be patient:** It may take an older dog time to learn that there are different house rules in her new home.

You may need help grooming your dog. Even dogs who go to a groomer will need touch-up work in between. How often and how much time you need to spend on grooming depends on your dog. A friend of ours has a Pekinese who needs daily grooming, but our Corgis can get by with once a week grooming unless they are shedding. Make sure that you check toenails, ears, and teeth at least every other week—weekly is better, plus it becomes part of your regular routine that way.

Training is, of course, one of the best parts of having a dog. Working together, learning new things, preparing for competitions, and so on is a blast! If your dog is shared with another family member, make sure that you both train the same way or divide up who does what. For example, you could train for obedience, while a sibling trains for agility. As always, make sure that you agree on what words to use and what they mean. We have had family confusion using the words "twirl" and "spin" for different spins—one clockwise, one counterclockwise. Since Kate was working the dogs on that more than Deb, Deb had to be retrained.

Exercising is another fun activity to do with your dog. Most dogs need some exercise every day. You need to establish who will give the dog a long walk and when. A game of fetch might be substituted, but make sure that your dog gets good exercise every day—for both her physical and mental health. It is good for you, too.

The Importance of Routine

Routines are very important to dogs. They like to know what to expect and often look forward to particular times of day (especially mealtimes). Dogs who don't have a routine are more prone to anxiety and are stressed more easily. There are a few dogs who get so upset when a routine is changed that they do better with a chaotic schedule—those are the rare ones, though.

Routines are also good for you; it's much easier to remember to walk your dog at noon if you have done so every day since you got her. Plus for situations like remembering medications, a set routine will help you stay on top of things.

Meals are very easy to put into a routine. In fact, if your dog gets breakfast at 7 A.M. every day, you will find that she will never let you forget. Our dogs get rawhide chewies at 9 P.M. every night. We know that it's almost 9 when Deb's Belgian Tervuren Hokey comes running to the nearest person and starts howling.

The Right Word

One of the most confusing commands for many dogs is Sit Down. Most dogs learn Sit and learn Down. When they hear "sit down," they often stand, looking at you and slowly wagging their tails, as they are quite confused. Do you want them to sit or to lie down? Try to avoid confusing situations like this.

Bedtime is another important part of your dog's routine. If you get up at 6 A.M. daily and go to bed at 9:30 P.M., your new dog will quickly adjust to your schedule. Do keep in mind that your dog has no idea that it is now summer vacation, the weekend, or a holiday. She will still expect to get up at 6 A.M. With time, she will learn to go back to bed and snuggle in with you until later. Tia, our Australian Shepherd, could happily sleep in at our house, but the Belgian Tervurens all want to rise and shine at dawn.

Don't expect a young puppy to sleep a full 8½ hours without needing to go out to pee. For the first week or so, you may have to get used to a 1 A.M. pee walk—or even more frequently. Many experts say to figure that a pup can go as many hours without a bathroom break as they are old in months—so a 2-month-old pup can go two hours, a 3-month-old pup three hours, and so on. While many puppies do better than that, it is a good guideline to keep in mind.

When your puppy gets older, she will be able to sleep through the night and will start waking up when you do. This schedule will also help with housetraining, since your pup will get used to going out to pee at a certain time in the morning and again at night. Your pup's daytime walks can also be fit into your routine—one after you shower, another before lunch, and so on.

Using a crate will greatly help in housetraining. Puppies prefer to sleep in and be in clean areas. With a crate, your pup will quickly start to make noise when she needs to go out as she does not want to be in a wet, pee-soaked area. Eventually your puppy will come to consider the entire house her area, and she will run to a door or ask you in some way to let her out. Clever canines can be taught to ring a bell by the door to alert you.

Some families will train their puppies to eliminate on papers or in a litter box—use a separate one if you have both dogs and cats or you may create

For Parents Only

The best part about having a dog who is technically your child's is that you don't have responsibility for the chores. Although you should expect to have to pitch in sometimes, this is a good opportunity for your child to learn responsibility and the importance of caring for a beloved friend. Kids who grow up with responsibilities and chores become responsible adults.

Cleaning up after a puppy who has had an accident will teach your child to watch the puppy more carefully—and as a side effect, introduce her to using a sponge, hygiene concerns after dealing with urine or stool, and a wide variety of cleaning techniques. Their future college roommates and any future spouses will appreciate these skills.

Having to deal with chewed-up toys or shoes will teach your child to pick up her things and again to be more observant of the dog. It also helps kids to establish priorities. What is more important—your chewed-up baseball hat or your beloved canine companion? No question, right?

Sometimes, a dog may destroy a beloved or valuable heirloom. You have to point out that a living being is still more important, even if the heirloom was yours. Counting to 100 or crying somewhere in private is a good idea in these cases.

Parents need to remember, however, that you are dealing with living beings who have needs that must be taken care of, and even responsible kids occasionally forget to check the dog's water bowl. You need to be an unobtrusive backup, making sure all the essentials are covered. And if you have more than one dog, you can split chores. We often have one person feeding the dogs at our home, while another person rinses and refills water bowls.

cat litter box problems. These dogs will still need to learn to go outside at some point, so why not just skip this step if possible?

There are certain times when you can predict your pup will need to go out. When she wakes up from a long sleep or even a nap, zip her outside. If she has been running around, playing wildly, and suddenly stops, out she goes. Within 20 minutes of eating, many dogs will need to go out. Pay close attention now, and your housetraining chores will be much easier.

Puppies from pet stores who have lived in crates and not been kept clean may be harder to housetrain—another good reason for getting your pup from a reputable breeder. Our dogs came from top-notch shelters or top breeders, and housetraining has been relatively easy and quick.

You should also set aside some time each day for training. While your puppy is young, she will have a very short attention span. Sometimes even five minutes can seem like an eternity. Older dogs can focus for longer periods of time, but keep training sessions fairly short and upbeat so that your dog will look forward to them every day. Multiple short training sessions are preferable to one long session. Training can be mixed right in with your care routine. Our dogs learn to sit for their dinner, spin or twirl for their chews, and wait at doors to go outside and play fetch.

A Clean Start Helps with Housetraining

A puppy or dog who has been raised in a clean environment will prefer to eliminate somewhere else—usually outside. Many breeders have two compartment puppy areas with shavings or some other absorbent bedding on one side to encourage the puppies to eliminate there. The mother dog will teach her pups to keep the main area clean.

Profile: Kate and Flash

I was 7 years old when I got Flash, my Pembroke Welsh Corgi. I had wanted a dog of my own, specifically a Corgi, for a couple of years. My mom said I had to wait until I was 7. Meanwhile she went to work looking for a good breeder. We needed a Corgi who would be a perfect companion for a kid.

We picked up Flash on Valentine's Day at just 10 weeks of age. Right from the start, she was wild and full of herself, chasing after our barn cat as soon as she got out of the car. Housetraining went easily, but my mom had to help out while I was in school. Flash slept in her crate in my room and also hung out with our other two dogs.

Flash learns quickly; she is almost too smart for her own good. She is very athletic and fast and can be impatient with me. It has been a lot of hard work with some setbacks, but we have accomplished many goals.

I cover most of Flash's care myself now, although when I was younger, Mom helped more with feedings, walks, and toenail trimmings. Plus my parents cover most of her expenses.

Herding was the easiest thing to train, as Flash has so much natural instinct. The hardest things have been teaching her to leave bars up and hit the contacts in agility. Flash and I have competed in herding, agility,

Kate and Flash.

obedience, tracking, rally, freestyle, and junior showmanship. We even do hiking and water work, along with carting and flyball for fun.

The main drawback to having a dog of my own is early morning walks. (Note from Deb: Kate is *not* a morning person!) Flash loves waking me up bright and early.

Flash is a very athletic dog with high drive and a strong will to work. She is an incredible partner, and we have achieved national honors, including being the first junior team to earn a Versatile Companion Dog title from the AKC. I realize how lucky I am to have had such a great friend for my very first dog. I have become spoiled—now I expect all dogs to be as talented and wonderful as Flash. As you can see in our photo, Flash thinks of herself as a *big* dog.

Flash is my best friend and a beloved member of our family. She even convinced my dad that Corgis are real dogs, and she is the mascot for our 4-H club. She is now 7 years old, and I hope we have many more years together.

3

Elementary School: Teaching Household Manners

Just as you learned many basic skills in elementary school, like arithmetic, writing, and reading, your new dog will need to learn basic skills that make him a fun addition to your household. These skills include positions such as sit and down, paying attention, and walking nicely.

Household Manners

As discussed in chapter 2, it is very important that your dog learn proper behavior around doorways. In most cases, you will want your dog to wait for you to go first through a doorway or simply wait and stay put while you open the door.

To start training for doorway behavior, you need your dog on a leash. The leash will help prevent your dog from zipping out the door. As you open the door, say "Stay" or "Wait." If your dog stays back, praise and give a treat. If he goes to zip through, use the leash to stop him and bring him back. A hand or foot put in front of your dog along with a "get back" works well, too. Please note, we are *not* saying to hit or kick your dog! Eventually, when you say "Get back" or "Wait," your dog will stop or even back up and remain in place. Don't forget to give lots of praise and some treats when he does it right!

Positive Training for Positive Results

It is important to praise and/or give your dog a treat when he does things right. Too often, we rush in with corrections but forget to reward the good behavior. This happens even more after your dog is trained and does things right most of the time. If you don't periodically remind your dog that he is doing the right thing, he may become confused and stop doing it. Besides, unexpected rewards are good for all of us—think how you glow when you get an unexpected "good job!"

Many a dog has been banished to the garage or an outside doghouse just for begging. The easiest way to deal with this problem is not to allow it to start. *Never* feed your dog scraps directly from the table. If you want to give your dog a special tidbit, take it over to his food bowl. This is one of those rules that the entire family must follow. One great treat from the table and your dog will dream of it forever—in a daydream accompanied by a string of drool.

Here's an example with one of our dogs. One day Kate accidentally dropped her entire pork chop right on the floor in front of Beep's face. He was thrilled with this gift from heaven but relinquished it when asked. Ever after, he chose to lay near Kate's chair at dinnertime.

Crazy Eights and Lunatic Syndrome are our descriptions of the wild "running through the house" behavior of many puppies and young dogs. These actions include looping around the kitchen table or the coffee table in the living room at a run, possibly dashing into the family room and banking off the back of the couch, or tearing through the house trailing a stream of toilet paper. Your dog may have his own version of these "crazies." These actions can be fatal to any breakable objects in the path of the runway. Although this may be cute in your little 8-week-old Papillon, think about an 8-month-old Saint Bernard puppy doing the same thing—not a pretty sight! The minute this behavior starts, you need to catch the offender and take him outside. Clearly your dog needs more exercise. Remember, a tired puppy is a good puppy!

Attention

Just as your teacher calls your class to attention before she starts up a new subject, so you need to get the attention of your puppy or dog before you can teach him anything. Learning to pay attention is a valuable skill that will make training much easier.

Hokey is showing the great attention you can train into your dog. He is trying to make eye contact, even though Deb has the camera in the way.

The goal here is to have your dog look at and focus on you. One easy way to start is with a treat. Show the puppy the treat and then bring it up to your eye and say "Watch" or "Look" or whatever word you choose. The young dog in our photo is just a year old. When the dog makes eye contact, say "good" or "yes" and give the treat. Dogs catch on to this *very* quickly. After all, eye contact is an important factor in dog pack behavior, and they are looking at their "leader" and even getting a reward for doing so!

Easy Attention Methods for Small Dogs

If you are teaching a very small dog or puppy, you can make attention training easier by kneeling on the floor or putting your dog on a safe raised surface. A rubber mat placed on a table will keep him from slipping and make it easier for him to look at you. Imagine how much easier it is to look at your dad's eyes than it is to look up at a skyscraper!

The next step is to move the treat off to the side, but the dog must still look at your eyes to earn the goody. Be patient; it will take your dog a few seconds, maybe even a minute, to figure this out. After your dog has this down pat, you can use this command in a variety of ways and places. As you walk by your dog lying on his bed, say "Watch." His eyes should come up to meet yours, and then you praise him or give him a treat. Attention training will be the basis of much of your work with your dog. Without it, you will often find it very frustrating to try and teach things to your dog.

The Three R's of Dog Training

For human pupils we talk about reading, 'riting, and 'rithmetic. For dogs, we have restraint, returning, and resting. Restraint is learning to Sit, Down, and Stand; returning is learning to Come; and resting is learning to Stay. These are basic necessities for a pleasurable companion. All of these things can easily be taught to a very young pup (we start our dogs right at 8 weeks), and despite folklore to the contrary, older dogs *can* learn new tricks, too.

Restraint (Sit, Down, and Stand)

Sit is the command most dogs seem to master first. Take a treat and hold it in front of your puppy's nose. Then raise the treat up and back a little. Your pup will automatically sit to raise his head up high. If he jumps up, just move the treat out of his reach. Virtually every dog will catch on to this in minutes unless they have a medical condition that makes it hurt to sit. As your dog sits, use the word "sit" (or whatever word you plan to use—dogs are flexible, and we know dogs who sit on a "park it" command) and praise and give the treat. If you repeat this process three times in a row, say five times a day, your dog will have Sit mastered within a week. You then need to wean off the treats so he doesn't always get one every time.

Down is a trickier command. Many dogs are uncomfortable lying down and being in a vulnerable position. Still, even puppies can learn this command. With your pup standing, take a treat and move it from in front of his nose down and back between his front legs. Support his rear so he doesn't just back up. To reach the treat he will need to lie down. In our photo, 4-month-old

Queezle knows the Down very well as she is lured with a treat. Eventually, she will be weaned off the treats.

Queezle shows a quick Down. Actually, the dogs seem to "fold back" into the Down. Some dogs may need to be helped into the down position. Make sure you use plenty of praise and treats when your dog does this.

Although many dogs go through life without knowing the Stand command, it can make your life easier—as well as make your veterinarian and groomer happier. To teach the Stand, have your pup sit. Then take a cookie by his nose and move it under his chin and straight back. Your pup will "kick back" his hind legs and stand to reach the treat. He may need a steadying hand under his abdomen at first.

Balancing Treats and Praise

Using treats and/or using a clicker (see our clicker resources in Appendix A) are valuable ways to let your dog know he is doing something right. However, you need to wean off these rewards so he does not become dependent on them. We all know dogs who check to see whether you have a treat before they obey. You want your stellar canine to obey even if you don't have food. So go heavy on the praise and light on the biscuits.

Returning (Come)

Coming when called is a skill that could save your dog's life. If he was heading for the road but turned and came back when you called, he would be safe. This is a command that must *always* be positive and 100 percent enforceable. The easiest way to start this is to have someone hold the pup while you go a short distance away. Have the person restrain him briefly as you encourage him to come. He will then burst out of the starting blocks and race to you. Be sure you make a big deal out of him when he comes!

Puppies love recall games where you take turns holding the pup and releasing him to the other person. This is a good game for the whole family to play with the puppy.

It is also important *not* to call your dog when you can't enforce it. If he is running pell-mell after a squirrel, the odds are he won't come to a sliding stop, spin, and dash back to you. So don't waste the breath hollering and teaching him that Come is a command he can ignore. Useful techniques are turning and running in the opposite direction so your dog suddenly wonders what wonderful thing *you* are chasing, or lying on the ground making strange noises so your dog comes to investigate. Do *not* chase your dog. Unless you are a track star, you probably won't be able to catch him, and dogs love chase games.

If your dog really seems to be having trouble with Come, let him drag a thin long line around the fenced yard. Parachute cord works well. Then, with gloves on to protect your hand, casually pick up the cord every now and then and call him. If he hesitates about coming, gently reel him in, all the

The Importance of Come

Coming when called should *always* be a good thing. *Never* call your dog and then give him a correction. If he has done something less than wonderful, go get him; don't call him to you. By the same token, if your pup enjoys running around the yard, don't always call him and immediately bring him inside. Call him, give him a treat, and let him run around some more. Otherwise, he will connect coming with having to go in and ending his fun.

while telling him how wonderful he is. Praise and treat when he gets to you, and then let him go play again. Most dogs start to think you have some special magic that always convinces them to come. Never leave your dog out alone with a dragging line, because he could get caught up on trees or bushes.

Resting (Stay)

It is very useful to have a dog who will stay on command as well. Don't start teaching this until your dog is solid on his basic Sit, Down, and Stand. What you want is a dog who will remain in place until you tell him otherwise. If you plan to do any competitions, your dog must also stay in the position you left him in. Put your dog in the position you want, and then put a hand in front of his nose and say "Stay." A second or two is all you will get at first, so be sure to give a treat right away. You may even want to step in front of him to block any movement. This is best taught on a leash. Hokey, the pup shown in the photo on page 29, was just 10 weeks old when he posed here. Gradually you can add time and distractions.

Repeatability, a Fourth R

Repeatability could be a fourth R for your dog. You need to be sure he will obey at home not only, but at other locations as well. Many pet stores allow dogs on leash in the store. These can be great locations to train in, and your dog learns that he needs to do what he is told no matter where he is. Plus, the staff are usually very willing to help you and even hand out some treats themselves.

Our dogs go to sports events, parks, and even band practice right from the start. A walk in the park can expose your dog to lots of new things. He will meet many different people and learn that he needs to obey no matter where he is or what fun things are going on around him.

Hokey shows that even a very young pup can start to learn commands such as Stand.

Walking Nicely

In school, *you* have hallway etiquette—walking quietly and calmly to your next class with no fooling around and no talking. For your dog, this means walking calmly on a leash without pulling or dragging you and not sniffing the whole way or chewing on the leash. At least, that is the ideal picture we all have in mind.

Although it may seem contradictory, it is easiest to start the walking practice off leash in a fenced yard or in the house. With your pup running happily around, you start walking yourself, carrying a treat in your left hand as it hangs down. When your pup comes over and sniffs the treat, he will fall into position by your left side—even if it is just for a second, give him the treat. This is a simple version of "choose to heel" (see the resources in the back of this book). Your dog will catch on quickly, and you will find that he keeps coming over to join you.

Meanwhile, you should get your pup used to wearing a collar and have him drag a lead around a bit so he is comfortable with that idea. Do not leave him alone with a dragging leash as he could get caught on things. Remember to have appropriate collars and leads. A 1-inch-thick nylon leash is *way* too heavy for a small breed. Rolled leather is always good for collars as it doesn't break or tangle the hair, and we prefer leather leads—as thin as ¼ inch—because they are easier on our hands.

Your pup is now choosing to walk by you. It is time to add the leash. Start in your yard. You may even want to follow your pup at first as he wanders around with the leash on. Then call him to your left and take a few steps. Don't forget praise and/or treats! When he is walking nicely in familiar places, you need to head out into the world. As you can see in the photo, a walk with an attentive dog on a loose leash is a pleasure.

Follow Through

It is important that you immediately reinforce your commands after you are sure your dog knows them. For example, if your dog knows "Sit," you should say it just once. Then, if he doesn't do it, help him into the position. We have all seen dogs who figure out that Sit doesn't need to happen until the fourth or fifth command.

When you start going to new places, expect that your pup may want to drag and sniff. Be patient. Our dogs have different words for when we want them to walk along and pay attention and for when they are free to sniff—but, hopefully, never to drag or pull! If your pup has a "bathroom" word, you can use that word when you stop at a suitable place on your walk.

Hokey has learned how to walk nicely and attentively using his watch, choose to heel, and being a tree techniques.

Why Heel on the Left?

Tradition has it that your dog should walk at your left side. Why, you ask? It is thought this tradition developed from the days of the knights. Since your horse was on your right side when you led him, your dog had to walk on the left to be out of the horse's way. And why, then, lead the horse on your right? This supposedly was due to most knights being right-handed, so they wore their swords on their left (easy to reach across their body). It is easier to mount a horse without having to swing the sword leg over the horse.

For new places, remember to use extra-special treats and lots of praise. You might also want to carry a beloved toy and use that for a reward. Still, your dog is going to pull at times. Now what? An effective technique is "being a tree:" the dog pulls, the person stops and pretends to be a 100-year-old oak tree, firmly planted in the ground. Don't even say anything; just quietly stand until your dog releases pressure on the leash. He may look back, take a step back, or simply relax. When the pressure is off, you start again. At first, it may take you forever to get anywhere. Still, if you are consistent with this technique, it does work. Your dog figures out that a loose leash means he gets to go new places, sniff new smells, and so on.

Putting It All to Use in Real Life

Many of you will argue that all the things you learn in school have no practical purpose. Your dog is lucky in that *his* training is practical. Your Sit, Down, and Stay all can help with doorway etiquette. If your dog is sitting and staying, he isn't running out the door. When a guest arrives, you can show off your dog's great behavior by having him Sit and Stay. Company can greet him by petting him gently, and no one is jumped on or frightened.

A Down Stay is the perfect way for your dog to join you at mealtimes but not beg or cause a commotion. Down Stays are also extremely helpful when you are waiting at the vet's office or when your dog is next to you while you watch TV. A Down Stay is a handy command while you fill the food bowl or trim toenails. If you travel to Europe, your well-trained dog will lie quietly at your feet while you enjoy a lemonade at an outdoor café!

The Stand is very helpful for your dog's groomer, as it is often easier to work on a standing dog and helpful for your veterinarian to do a physical examination. Plus, the Stand makes it easier for you to brush your dog.

If you work at it, you can come up with many places where you can put your dog's basic commands to use in real life.

Special Equipment

Although you have your basic new-puppy equipment, there are additional items that may help you enjoy your dog to the max:

- **Retractable leashes:** Although these can be excellent for exercising your dog in places where he can't safely go off leash, they do encourage your dog to pull, as there is always some pressure, and the thin cords can be dangerous. Never let a dog on a leash like this around a corner or out of sight where you can't tell what he is doing.
- **Prong collars:** These collars look like something out of a medieval torture catalog. For a dog with a very strong pulling tendency—such as a sled dog breed—think of this type of collar as power steering. You don't correct or jerk your dog with this—just stick to your tree imitation and your dog will correct himself. These collars can be especially helpful with adolescent dogs.
- **Head halters:** These contraptions fit on a dog's head like a halter on a horse. The theory behind them is that you need to control only the head and aren't fighting the strong muscles of the dog's neck and chest. They work well for dogs with sensitive tracheas as well. Most dogs need a little time to happily adjust to wearing these. Use liberal amounts of treats and praise.
- **Harnesses:** Harnesses may work well for small dogs or dogs with sensitive tracheas. With larger dogs, however, a harness makes it even easier to pull. Save these for skijoring!

Profile: Jamie and Buddy

Jamie is a top 4-H member who is heading off to college to train as a veterinary technician. While she will miss her parents and her horse, she will *really* miss her White German Shepherd Dog, Buddy.

Jamie was 13 years old when Buddy entered her life. She was very upset and grieving over the loss of her elderly Lab mix, so her parents took her to the local shelter to look at dogs. Jamie found the perfect dog—at least the perfect dog for her! Many people would have avoided the large adolescent dog. Most dogs turned in to shelters are intact males between the ages of 6 and 12 months. Buddy was on his way to becoming a sad statistic when Jamie showed up.

Jamie found true love in a gangly adolescent White German Shepherd Dog who became her best buddy!

Buddy was old enough that housetraining was not a huge problem. Jamie assumed all his care, though her parents chipped in for veterinary bills. Still, that left Jamie walking, feeding, training, and loving this big guy. As Jamie says, "The only thing I had help with was the vet bills, but other than that, he is and always will be my responsibility."

Because Buddy was a bit older, he came with some problems and habits already established. He has a bit of separation anxiety and is not comfortable being in a crate. Buddy is very smart and, like many herding dogs, wants to work with his person. Still, Jamie has worked long and hard to make him the canine gentleman he is today.

Teaching Buddy to Come was easy as he was thrilled to have a girl of his own. Working on heeling off leash for obedience competitions was harder—Buddy alternated between going to visit people and simply running out of the ring. Still Jamie persisted, and today, Buddy has his AKC CD (Companion Dog) title, his AKC RN (Rally Novice), APDT Rally Level 1, CGC (Canine Good Citizen), and Therapy Dog certification.

Buddy also does agility and junior showmanship with Jamie as well as altered conformation. Jamie wants to add Schutzhund to their talents in the future.

Jamie feels the primary drawback to having a dog of your own is the expense—vet bills, food, and toys all add up. Still, it is worth it to her.

Jamie feels Buddy is special because "I believe that he knows what I am thinking. He does things for me before I ask him. If a dog from the shelter can give so much love and laughs in my life, then he is very special to me!"

Since many people are not familiar with White German Shepherd Dogs, Jamie and Buddy are ambassadors for the breed. Jamie enjoys educating people about this rare breed. As you can see in their photo, Jamie and Buddy are truly best buddies.

One fault Buddy does have is whining in the car. Jamie sums this up using a quote from Dave Barry—"Dogs feel very strongly that they should always go with you in the car, in case the need should arise for them to bark violently at nothing right in your ear." Still, some noise pollution is nothing compared to the love and devotion of her four-footed friend!

For Parents Only

One thing you will find is that most parents who train dogs have well-trained, well-behaved children. The same techniques of positive reinforcement that work so well with dogs work great on kids, too. Give your dog the chance to make the right choice, as in walking by your side, and then reward him by allowing him to think for himself; you are right there to help him make the right choice if he has trouble. This principle also works with kids—letting them think things out for themselves, but being available for backup if needed.

Although food treats like liver biscuits may not be so hot for your kids, privileges like getting to stay up a half hour later work well. I don't suggest using a prong collar, but a retractable leash would have worked well when my kids were toddlers. And leather clothing *is* all the rage in certain circles!

I found that from early on, my kids responded to my dog commands when I forgot and gave them a Stay command, complete with hand signal. There was the embarrassing time when Kate was about 5 years old and told me in no uncertain terms that I didn't need to use my "dog training voice" on her. Still, they Come, Sit, Down, and Stay fairly reliably and will walk with me nicely.

4

Avoiding Detention

Even though we all hope to have the perfect puppy or dog, the reality is that most dogs will have some problems at least some of the time. Your job is to try to prevent problems from developing and, if they develop, nip them in the bud. If you have done a thorough job of teaching the basics, problems are less likely to start up and are easier to fix if they do occur. So, hopefully, you did your homework and you will both avoid detention.

Developing Respect for (Human) Authority

Although you hope your dog is your best friend, or at least one of your best friends, you are still the one in charge. As the responsible partner, you need to have a relationship with your dog that is fun and loving but still has an element of respect. Think of how you relate to your parents.

Dogs between 6 and 15 or 18 months of age usually go through about a six-month stage when they are terrible. Think of it as the teenage, juvenile delinquent stage. Your perfect puppy suddenly ignores your commands, chews things, and is a total brat. Be patient, increase her exercise, and continue with daily training lessons, keeping her on leash if need be. This stage will pass, but most dogs left at shelters are dogs in this age category. Realize the hassles your parents have with teenage humans and show some sympathy.

Your dog needs to obey when you tell her to do something and to show appropriate behavior around her toys, food, and places like the bed. You should be able to take toys from your dog and even reach into her food bowl. Trading works well if she is hesitant to give up stolen or inappropriate toys. She learns that giving up objects to you results in something even better coming her way. For food bowl guarding, start by putting your hand in her bowl with some treats. She needs to eat from your hand, and she is learning that your hand by the bowl is a good thing. Occasionally, adding treats to her bowl while she is eating reinforces to your dog that your hand near her dish is a positive thing.

We discussed bed rules earlier, and this includes any "place guarding." Although your dog is a beloved member of the family, she is a minor member. If you want the bed or the couch, your dog should get off when told. If she does not, you will need to go back to step one and not allow her on any furniture. Booby trapping can help when you aren't around to watch closely. Some dogs are put off by something as simple as aluminum foil on a chair seat, and there are commercial "scat mats," which use a mild electrical current. Creative families may set up empty soda cans with a few pennies taped inside as a noise deterrent.

Possession Is Not Always Nine-Tenths of the Law

If your dog gets very possessive about a certain toy, even to the point of growling at you, it may be best to simply get rid of that toy. You can try trades first, using special treats and then returning the toy to her, but if she persists in being aggressive about a possession, simply get rid of it.

Big dogs often figure out that the really good people food is kept on counters or in cupboards. Some may try to raid these storage areas. For cupboards, the locks used for babies work very well. Placing a small mousetrap on the counter can discourage counter surfing. This way, your dog won't be hurt, but will get quite a surprise and will hopefully give up her scavenging. This works better than guarding the counter yourself, because she won't receive the correction from you and will think that there is a monster living on the counter. For a little dog who gets on the table to help herself to your midnight snack, be sure to keep chairs pushed in or booby trap the edges of the table. Empty soda cans with a few pennies inside and then taped over make a great crash when lined up along counters. When the snooping hound tries to counter surf, the resulting racket often stops the behavior.

Dogs may jump up on people for many reasons. It may just be cheerful exuberance. It can be to try and make eye contact. It can also be a way of showing slight dominance. No matter what the reason, your dog should only jump up on people if invited to do so. Dogs quickly learn who will allow this behavior and who won't. The best way to deal with this behavior is to prevent it from happening. Start your pup off learning to greet people properly.

If jumping-up behavior is established, it can be hard to get rid of. *Everyone* must be consistent about not allowing your dog to jump up unless invited—and with some dogs, it works best simply not to allow jumping up on anybody. Dogs who jump up can be discouraged by a gentle intercepting push or by moving toward the dog, which puts her off balance. For some dogs, grabbing her paws gently and holding her up will discourage her. Most dogs want simply to jump and move off, so they are unhappy being held up. You can also set your dog up, with her on a leash, and have someone approach. As she goes to jump, give her a correction and, at the same time, give her a command such as Sit. Then praise her for the Sit.

One of the first signs of dog adolescence seems to be not coming when called. Don't panic or overreact—your dog is simply testing her wings. If your dog doesn't come when called—and we mean come when called the very first time—you have a number of remedial options. You can run the other way, lie down and make strange noises, or quietly walk your dog down. You may have to try all three variants. When your dog does come, quietly put her on lead or gently take her by the collar. You do *not* want to correct her for finally coming, but you don't want to praise her, either. She needs to be reminded that she must come on the first call.

Substitution versus Correction

It is important that along with discouraging bad behaviors we provide our dogs with good substitute behaviors. Using a Sit for greeting and praising your dog for the Sit will get faster and more consistent results than simply correcting the jumping.

Now that you are aware you have this problem, you need to take some action. For the next few weeks—yes, it may take that long or even longer—your dog is on a leash or a line at all times, the exception being a fenced area on your property where she can run. If she is in that area, do not call her, as you can't enforce the command. You will need to wait until she comes to you or the door. It helps to put her on a long line to drag around the yard. Never leave her alone with a dragging line, but hang out outside with her, maybe reading a good dog book, while she putters around. Every now and then, call her after putting your foot on the line. If she comes, great! Make a big fuss over her. If she doesn't come, calmly reel her in and give her a quiet pat. Then let her go off to explore again.

When you are having problems with the Come, you may need to start using really good treats. Small pieces of cooked chicken or beef can brighten up a relationship big time! Eventually you need to test the recall. Do this in a fenced area, and if your dog doesn't come right away, ignore her and go back to the line work.

Playing Well with Others: The Social Dog

Ideally, we all want a dog who is friendly with both people and other dogs. Unfortunately, this is not always the case. Certain breeds tend to be friendlier than others, but training and socialization are *extremely* important. Genetics plays a part here, too—some breeds and some individual dogs are simply friendlier right from the start.

Hopefully, you were able to have some temperament testing done on your dog or puppy, so you chose a middle-of-the-road, outgoing canine. The mother of your dog is also very important, not just for her genetic temperament but also because she has influenced how your pup sees the world for the first eight weeks of your dog's life. If the mother is friendly and likes people, she will set that example for her puppies.

A good breeder or top shelter will arrange socialization for the dogs and puppies in their care. Encouraging people of different ages and appearances to meet the dogs and play with them is very important. It is also important for dogs to have contact with other canines during those first eight weeks so that they learn proper social behaviors. A singleton pup is at a distinct disadvantage since she won't have siblings to interact with. Breeders often arrange to "borrow" a pup to play with their singletons.

After your puppy or dog comes home with you, it becomes *your* job to continue that socialization. You need to expose your pup to a wide range of experiences, taking care that she is not frightened or overwhelmed in the process. This might mean going to watch soccer practice, going to pick up kids after school, and visiting pet-friendly pet stores. A good puppy kindergarten class is an excellent way for an "only dog" to meet other canines.

Providing Backup

Be a good role model! If your pup is frightened or overwhelmed by a situation, do *not* baby-talk her. Simply say it's OK, encourage her to continue on, and basically ignore whatever was bothering her. Sometimes, you can encourage her to approach scary things such as umbrellas, but if not, simply ignore and continue on as if nothing was worrisome.

Carry treats with you at all times. You can hand them to people you meet, and they can give them to your pup. She will learn that people are wonderful treat dispensers. This is an excellent place to practice your proper greeting behavior, too—have your pup sit to earn the treats.

Realize that not all dogs will like one another. After all, you aren't friends with everyone you meet, either! Still, your dog must learn to tolerate other dogs and behave in their presence. As you can see in the photo on page 39, some dogs become good buddies. A good dog obedience class is an excellent place for you both to work through this.

Some dogs will happily run around with other dogs but will guard their food and/or their toys. If you have a single dog household, simply pick up food and toys when a doggie friend comes over. It makes life much simpler.

If you have more than one dog, they will often play together happily as Tia and Queezle do.

Separation Anxiety—Home Alone

We want our dogs to enjoy being with us, and we like having them around us. Still, there are times when your dog will have to handle being left home alone. Ideally, this will be for only short periods of time. Once she is grown and can hold her bladder, there will be days when your dog may be left alone for as long as eight hours or so.

Many dogs simply curl up and go to sleep. Others will happily watch the neighborhood or the local squirrels out the window. A few will settle with a chew toy. However, there are some dogs who feel really uncomfortable being left alone. These dogs may bark, chew in frustration, destroy things, or even lick or chew on themselves. What now?

Dogs with ingrained separation anxiety or who have had a great deal of stress may need a consultation with a veterinary behaviorist and possibly even some behavior modifying drugs. Still, many dogs manage to overcome this problem with a little effort on your part.

Leaving the radio or TV on—pick talk shows, classical music, or nature shows, not wild rock and roll—provides some comfort noise for your dog. There are even special videos made to amuse your dog.

Since your voice is one of your dog's favorite noises, you can also arrange to call home periodically and leave a message on your phone's answering machine. This could include tips like "Good dog. Quiet now. Lie down. Good dog!" For a dog with a destructive bent, saying things like "Leave it!

Tia relaxes happily with a peanut butter stuffed chew toy.

Be good!" might also be helpful. A truly destructive dog may need to stay in a crate or kennel while you are away—both for her safety and the safety of your house.

Audio books are all the rage. You might want to tape a training book so your dog can practice while you are away. Just hearing you read a book out loud may be soothing to your dog. The tape can be set to replay as needed.

Dogs who are food hounds can benefit from toys with food treats inside that the dog must work at to remove. Stuffing peanut butter or squeeze cheese into an old bone or Kong® toy is another idea to occupy your forlorn buddy. An example of a good chew item is shown in our photo.

Most dogs who have separation anxiety get upset right after you leave or shortly before they expect you home. It is best to make your departures and returns quiet times—even though you really want to give your dog an exuberant greeting. Quietly setting a routine and even ignoring your dog for a few minutes right when you get home can be helpful. And don't act too upset yourself when you leave!

Of course, adding another pet may help as well. It doesn't necessarily need to be a dog—many dogs are great friends with the family cat. Just make sure that your new pet doesn't come with separation anxiety, too.

Chewing: The House, Not Gum

First, you need to realize that chewing is a perfectly normal behavior for dogs. They chew to eat, they chew to relax, they chew while teething, they

Baloo enjoys chewing the hose, but this leads to a leaky hose. Not a good choice!

chew in frustration—you get the idea. And as you can see in our photo, they also chew for fun. There are a few sainted dogs who go through life without destroying anyone's beloved possessions, but they are few and far between, and we haven't met one yet. So accept that your dog will want and need to chew. Try to channel this urge in acceptable ways.

Puppies chew while teething just as human babies chew and drool. Cool objects are often preferable at this stage, so keep chew toys in the freezer or give your dog an ice cube to chew on and play with. The photo on page 42 shows some choices for your dog.

- **Gumabones:** Soft, rubbery chew toys that work well for teething pups with sore gums.
- **Veggies:** Raw carrots are favorites, although they can be messy.
- **Rubber chew toys:** There are a number of rubber chew toys that are virtually indestructible and that can be made very attractive by filling them with treats or smearing peanut butter or cheese on them. These toys give your puppy or dog a safe outlet for chewing and keep your possessions safe.
- **Marrowbones:** Make sure that these are long enough that they won't get caught on your dog's jaw. Clean some of the marrow out, as most dogs don't need that much extra fat, and throw these bones out after a few days. As the bone dries out, it will become hard and brittle. Pieces can break off and cause problems if your dog swallows

Which of these three things is not a good dog chew toy? If you guessed the slipper, you are right!

them. Some dogs even break teeth while chewing on bones. *Never* feed chicken or pork bones, especially if they have been cooked. They splinter easily. Even if you are feeding a raw diet, it is best to grind the chicken bones up.

- **Rawhide:** In various forms, flavors, and sizes, rawhide is extremely popular with the canine set. Although most dogs handle an occasional chew with no problem, discuss the proper size and how frequently your dog should have one with your veterinarian. Sticking to plain rawhide, ideally made in the United States for lower disease risk, is a good idea.
- **Pig ears and cow hooves:** These treats have a lot of fat, and hooves often splinter off and cause intestinal problems. Beware of these chew items!
- **Old shoes:** Many jokes center around old shoes for your dog. Don't fall into this trap! Your puppy has no way to tell the difference between your new expensive shoes and an old sneaker. Dog toys are a much better bet.

If nothing else, having a puppy teaches everyone in the family to pick up their things. We have

Beware Squeakers!

Although there are many very cute stuffed dog toys, remember that most of them have plastic squeakers inside. Dogs are skilled at toy surgery, removing fluff and squeakers faster than a plastic surgeon could remove extra fat! Make sure that you observe any toy destruction and pick up the squeakers and spare fluff. Don't give your dog stuffed animals made for children unless you remove the dangerous eyes or other plastic attachments first.

had dogs choose books, toys, furniture—although the only tooth marks on the kitchen chairs are from Kate as a baby!—and boots as chew objects. Remember, you can't really blame the dog—she doesn't know any better.

When you do find your dog chewing on something you don't want her to have, do *not* chase her! Instead, have an appropriate toy or chew item with you and offer her a trade. Treats work well for trading, also. Most dogs think the trading game is quite fun.

Too Much to Say: The Barker

There are some dogs who will bark no matter what you do. Certain breeds—think scenthounds or some sled dogs, for example—are almost genetically programmed to speak their minds freely. Small dogs and Terriers also tend to give their opinions on just about everything. So if you love peace and quiet, start out with a quiet breed such as a Saluki.

If your dog is definitely talking out of turn, you need to figure out why she is noisy. Some dogs bark as part of their "watchdog" heritage—alerting you to any strangers or changes in their environment. Of course, to a Shetland Sheepdog, a leaf blowing down the street may be considered significant. Most dogs learn to control their "alarm" barking if you simply go to them, tell them how good they were to alert you, and then give them a Quiet command. When they feel you have taken control of the situation, they relax.

The Silent Dogs?

Basenjis are spoken of as "barkless" dogs. However, this does not mean that they are "silent" dogs—they yodel, chirp, and moan with the best of them. Within any breed, you will have noisy dogs and quiet dogs.

If you will be away during the day, it makes sense to close curtains or put your dog in a room where she will not be observing the neighborhood, alerting and getting herself worked up all day long.

Some dogs can be taught both to bark on command and to be quiet. To teach the bark, get your dog excited and when she barks, say "Speak" or whatever word you want to use. Praise and treat when she does. Then, after she barks, say "Quiet" and praise and treat for the silence. After she barks reliably on command, you simply ignore any bark that wasn't asked for. You can then say "Quiet" and praise her when she complies. This does work for some dogs; others simply figure the Bark command gives them extra chances to sound off!

Loneliness is another reason for barking or howling. A dog sitting outside by a doghouse howling is a sad sight. This outside noise is also more likely to bother your neighbors than a dog barking inside a house. Try not to leave your dog outside alone if possible. If she acts lonely when left inside your house, check out the separation anxiety tips to keep her happy.

There are also those dogs who get so excited when working that they bark—this includes dogs who bark at their handlers when they are frustrated because their handlers are too slow or inconsistent. Agility dogs are known for this. They tell their handlers to speed up, get out of the way, shut up, and so on. For training class, a mouthful of peanut butter can restore peace and quiet on a short-term basis. One technique for a dog who barks while working is to stop and give her a treat when she barks. Yes, that sounds counter-productive, almost as if you are rewarding her for the noise. However, with many dogs, the treat seems to break the bark cycle and distract them so they focus back on the task at hand. Another technique is to put your dog in her crate for a time-out when she starts barking. Losing the chance to play can be devastating for some dogs, and they learn to be quiet so they can play longer.

High-Tech Solutions

There are special collars made to help control barking. Some of these work with a mild electric current such as the underground fence concept. Others use a citronella spray to distract and discourage the dog. Many of these collars can be adjusted so your dog gets one "free" bark—useful to let you know if there is an intruder before the collar reacts.

Admittedly, our own dogs bark a bit more than necessary at times. However, when the houses on our road were vandalized, every house within sight of our dogs—who occasionally bark about unusual things at the neighbors'—was left untouched. Nuisance barking is just that, but sometimes barking is a dog's way of conveying important information.

Dogs and Gardens

Cheryl Smith is the author of *Dog Friendly Gardens, Garden Friendly Dogs*. She suggests, "Make being in the approved spot a really good experience. The more consistent you are in your supervision and encouragement to dig only where you direct, the sooner the dog will get the idea." Cheryl's advice has saved many a formal garden from devastation and many a digging pooch from rehoming.

For Parents Only

The adolescent dog is *very* similar to the adolescent human. Your teenager may now find out what it is like to deal with a teenager. As with humans, patience and humor go a long way toward retaining a good relationship. I firmly believe that plenty of exercise is important, too.

This is a time when consistency and firmness pay big dividends. You need to be available to back your child up if the dog is having big problems and make sure that everyone is aware that "tough love" is still love. The "nothing for free" theory works well here, too. The dog must obey and be a decent canine citizen to earn privileges like extra treats or play time with a favorite toy.

It can be hard for kids to be totally consistent, so you need to be around to help supervise when they are working through a problem with the dog. Of course, *you* need to follow all the rules, too!

While adolescent dogs can be frustrating, they tend to be very enthusiastic, eager to try out new things, and excited about being with you most of the time. Try to capitalize on those good traits and take advantage of that extra energy. This might be a good time for the whole family to start hiking or skijoring!

Excavating: When Your Dog's a Digger

Although your dog may be a budding anthropologist or paleontologist, most likely you do not want her digging holes all over the lawn. For a dog, digging holes is fun, not a punishment as in Louis Sachar's book *Holes*. Even families who aren't heavily into landscaping don't appreciate craters scattered throughout the yard. We have to admit, though, these holes can be handy for planting bulbs for a natural look in springtime.

Again, you need to realize that some dogs and some breeds are more likely to dig than others. After all, Terriers were bred for many generations to "go to ground." That doesn't mean hidden identities; it means digging into the ground, dirt flying everywhere, in an attempt to catch their prey. And check out the paws on Dachshunds—those feet were made for digging!

Most families end up going one of two ways on the digging problems: You can do everything possible to prevent any digging, or you can set up a special place where your dog is allowed and encouraged to dig.

To prevent digging, *you* need to be watching your dog virtually 100 percent of the time when she is outside. The very minute dirt starts to fly, rush over and discourage and distract her. Having toys that she can play with outside will help. Keeping her well exercised—you can substitute "tired" here—will leave her without all that energy to burn.

Some people have claimed success by putting poop in old holes and then covering it with dirt. If your dog goes to dig there again, presumably she is disgusted and will give up digging forever. You can also fill holes with water. In our household, that would simply mean a wet, muddy dog instead of a merely dirty one. Many dogs simply shift their excavating urges to a new site when one is compromised.

The alternative—giving your dog a digging spot of her own—is gaining more advocates. After all, you get to dig in *your* garden, so why shouldn't she get to dig, too? To do this, it is best to mark off an area by raising it or putting a boundary around it. Remember, dogs learn things associated with places very quickly. In this area, put some sand or loosely compacted dirt. Burying a few biscuits near the surface will get your dog interested in digging. You can put fresh treats or toys in the area to keep her interest up.

Profile: Margo and Raisin

Margo got her Standard Poodle, Raisin, when Margo was 11 years old. Margo saw an ad for Raisin in the newspaper, and her family contacted the owners. Raisin was an older dog, and Margo's family was her third home. Margo is now 15, and they think that Raisin is 12, although they don't know for sure. Raisin and Margo have a great bond, as you can tell from their photo.

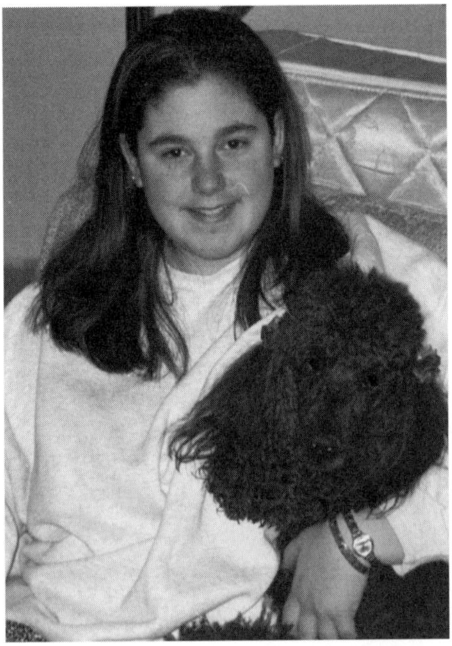

Raisin and Margo are a top 4-H team and best friends!

Raisin is very smart and eager to learn, so Margo had no trouble training her. Because she was an older dog, Raisin had a longer attention span than a puppy would have. When Margo first started 4-H, she was very quiet and shy. Working with her wonderful canine partner has given Margo more confidence and self-esteem. Margo and Raisin quickly moved up the ranks in 4-H to become one of the top teams. Margo and Raisin now give demos and help teach beginners.

They also compete in AKC Obedience, and Raisin has earned titles in both obedience and rally. Margo and Raisin have a number of high-scoring Junior awards in obedience. They have also been certified for therapy work.

Margo found that teaching Raisin to do junior showmanship was very easy. Raisin is a natural showgirl! Agility proved more difficult, and since Raisin is getting up there in years, Margo doesn't plan to compete with her, although they still sometimes do it for fun.

Margo enjoys being a dog owner and is Raisin's primary caretaker, although her mom helps her with some of the jobs and also covers expenses. Margo feels that the main drawback to having a dog is having to pick up after her.

Raisin is Margo's best friend. Margo says, "My relationship with Raisin is the best thing in the world. I don't think that there's a word that fits our relationship." Certainly Margo's friends and family have seen the benefits of her partnership with Raisin!

5

Health Class: Care and Feeding

Making your dog a member of your family means careful attention to his diet, exercise, grooming, and veterinary care. The entire family will participate in some aspects of your dog's care, while you alone might have responsibility for one area, such as grooming. Remember, every dog is an individual. You need to work with your veterinarian, groomer, and breeder or shelter to make sure you are giving your dog the best care possible.

Nutrition: Chow for the Hound

Although dogs are basically carnivores, most of them eat more like omnivores or scavengers. Dogs enjoy berries, fruits, and some veggies, as well as meat. Dogs need protein, fat, carbohydrates, fiber, vitamins, and minerals in their diet just like you do. Different dogs have different nutritional needs that can vary with age, breed, and size. Dogs who are older and less active have different nutritional needs than young, growing, very active puppies. Large-breed puppies have different requirements for growth than Toy-breed puppies. The important thing is to give your dog a balanced diet that is customized to fit his needs.

Water is the most important nutrient your dog needs. Although he may be able to go without eating for days, he should have fresh, clean water available all the time. Do not let him drink from toilets or stagnant ponds.

Water Safety

If there is a boil-water order issued for your family's drinking water, make sure that you boil enough for your dog, too. Also, if you camp, filter or chlorinate his drinking water just like you do for yourself so that he won't get any parasites.

Customizing the diet for your dog may be as simple as adjusting how many cups of kibble you give him each day. Remember that the amounts listed on bags of food are simply guidelines—most dogs should be fed less than what the bag indicates. Dogs with special needs, such as health problems like diabetes, may do best with diets prescribed by your veterinarian. Some dogs thrive on home-cooked meals.

Most dogs do very well on kibble diets. Look for foods with meat proteins listed near the top of the ingredient list and that don't have "split carbohydrates" such as corn meal, corn gluten, and so on. Discuss with your veterinarian which is the best food for your dog. Your breeder can tell you what food or foods your dog ate as a puppy and what foods her adult dogs do well on. Some breeds, such as Dalmatians, have special dietary needs (see the sidebar below).

Some dogs have problems with certain carbohydrates, such as wheat or corn. These grains can cause diarrhea, weight loss, and poor coats and health in susceptible dogs. Also, just like people, dogs can be allergic to certain foods. You may need to search out a diet that is free from certain ingredients if your dog has problems. Luckily, there are many foods to choose from these days—even exotic combos like duck and potato.

Kibble foods give your dog some chewing and are easy to feed. Dogs eating kibble may drink more than dogs eating canned food, as the food is drier. Some people add water to the food bowl. Canned food is more expensive and messier. However, dogs do love canned foods, and sometimes a compromise can be worked out in which you mix a little canned in with the regular kibble. If you choose to home-cook meals for your dog, you need to search out balanced and complete recipes. You can also contact the nearest

Special Dietary Needs

Dalmatians have problems with uric acid metabolism. Although you don't need to know the biochemistry, it is important to take care with certain proteins in a Dalmatian's diet to avoid the formation of bladder stones. Bedlington Terriers have trouble with copper metabolism, so their diets need to be carefully balanced for that mineral. Research whether your dog's breed has special dietary needs.

veterinary college to have a nutritionist evaluate the meals you make. Some recipe books have meals that are balanced for both you and your dog so you can all eat the same thing for supper.

Begging is not a good habit to encourage.

A recent trend is to feed dogs raw food, including raw chicken with bones, turkey necks, and so on. This can be a dangerous practice because bacteria such as Salmonella may be spread to you and your dog during food preparation and consumption. Bone splinters can cause serious injuries. If you are convinced that this is the right route for you, carefully balance the diet with a veterinary nutritionist and be extremely conscientious in your food preparations. Freeze-dried foods may be safer to use. Meat alone is *not* a balanced diet, so be sure to mix in some vegetables with your dog's supper. Your dog may need a calcium supplement for a balanced diet as well, if he is eating mainly raw meat.

Supplements should be used only after talking to your veterinarian. Too much of some nutrients can be dangerous. For example, adding extra calcium to your dog's diet, especially with a puppy or older dog, can be very bad. Brittle or deformed bones or kidney failure could result from a calcium imbalance. Calcium does not help cartilage, so if your puppy's ears don't stand up, adding extra calcium won't help. Still, some supplements can be helpful to your dog. For example, adding a chondroitin sulfate source or glucosamine supplement may be beneficial for a dog with arthritis.

We have discussed the problems with feeding your dog from the table, such as begging and food stealing. As you can see in the photo, begging dogs are a nuisance. Too many table scraps can contribute to a chubby dog or cause stomach upsets. Many human foods have more salt than your dog needs. If food isn't suitable for you to eat, it isn't suitable for your dog to eat, so don't give him the moldy cheese. If you want to give him a small piece of cooked chicken or a piece of steak, carry it out to his food bowl.

Although most families are careful about the food they feed their dogs, it is easy to forget that training treats should be healthy foods, too. Red dyes, high salt, and extra preservatives may add up to less than ideal snacks for your dog. And if your dog has food allergies, his treats need to be carefully chosen. Plus, many treats are high in calories. Most dogs will happily work for a small piece of their regular kibble. If your dog tends toward the chubby side, you can make him work for part of his meals. Our dogs happily Spin, Twirl, and Down for a mere piece of kibble.

Exercise: Run, Spot, Run!

Exercise is important for all dogs—from young puppies to elderly companions. Obesity is a major problem in pet dogs, and exercise is one of the ways to combat it. Exercise can help with behavior problems as well—a tired dog is a good dog. It is important to tailor the amount and type of exercise to your individual dog. A 10-mile hike is great for your Siberian Husky but might be a bit much for your Pekingese. Exercise is good for you, too. Walking or hiking, running agility, and throwing a ball all give *you* exercise as well as your dog. The whole family can make it a habit to enjoy a nice walk in the evening together.

Some dogs mimic the Energizer Bunny. Those dogs can run, leap, or swim for hours and still have energy to spare. Other dogs enjoy a short walk and then happily settle on the couch. Your dog's breed, age, and health status can all influence the amount and type of exercise he needs and wants. A young Border Collie may be happiest working sheep for a couple of hours, while an older Border Collie might be content with a 1-mile stroll down the lane. If your dog has a sudden drop in energy, you may need to look for a health problem.

With a young puppy, you need to remember that his bones are still growing. Bones grow from growth plates at the ends. If those growth plates are damaged, the bone will stop growing. This could leave your dog with one leg shorter than the others or twisted legs. To prevent serious damage, it is important not to encourage your puppy to do a lot of jumping. One accepted guideline is never to let your pup jump anything higher than his elbow until after a year of age. This includes leaping to catch balls or flying discs.

Older dogs may also need exercise restrictions. Due to arthritic changes, older dogs may be best off with low jumps (or no jumps at all), walks instead of runs, and less exercise overall. Still, even older dogs need and enjoy some daily exercise. Remember, as your dog's energy level and exercise time decrease, you will need to adjust his diet.

If you and your dog decide to embark on a joint exercise program, you need to start gradually. Just as the track coach makes you stretch, warm up, and cool down, you need to think about those things for your dog. Long walks,

Exercise Requirements Vary

Although Greyhounds appear to be marathon runners, in reality, they are sprinters. So the average Greyhound may dash about the yard wildly for five minutes or do a half-mile walk, and then he is ready to relax for the rest of the day. Dalmatians, on the other hand, were bred to run for hours alongside their master's horse or carriage. Research your breed!

Cautions for Short Muzzles

Dogs with shortened muzzles, such as Pugs and Bulldogs, have a very difficult time dealing with hot, humid weather. You may need to cut back on their exercise in the summer, or you can always purchase a doggie treadmill to set up in your air-conditioned living room. If you have asthma, this option might be better for you, too.

as shown in the photo, are great exercise. Many dogs learn to stretch for a treat, and simply luring your dog to reach to both sides for a treat will stretch many muscles. If you jog with your dog, start slowly so both of you can warm up your muscles. If you have a safe place to run with your dog off leash, remember that your dog will cover more ground than you—running off to explore and circling you with delight. When you return home, give your dog multiple small drinks instead of letting him gulp a large amount of cold water all at once. Walk part of the way home so that he doesn't go directly from running full tilt to standing around.

Walking is good exercise for both of you!

Keep in mind that heat can be devastating to your dog. Dogs sweat only via their pads and also cool off by panting. In hot, humid weather, evaporation rates are slow, and your dog can easily overheat. Most dogs will continue to run even if they are overheated just to stay with you, so it is your responsibility to make sure he is OK. If you are running in hot weather, carrying water for your dog to drink is a good idea. Also, while you have running shoes on, be aware that your dog's feet are in direct contact with hot pavement or sharp rocks. Choose the time of day and place you run carefully with your dog's safety in mind. Some dogs may need to wear booties to protect their feet.

Safety first! Along with dealing with heat, there are other considerations to keep your dog safe while exercising. If you work off leash somewhere, make sure he has identification on. Carry water on hot days and even in cold weather if your dog will be exerting himself. If you walk along roads that have been treated for ice in the winter, make sure that you rinse his paws afterward so that he won't lick any dangerous chemicals.

Some exercise can be stressful on bones and joints. Although an athletic Australian Shepherd can leap after an airborne disc as if he is flying, a Mastiff attempting the same feat could be headed for a cruciate ligament tear. Make the exercise appropriate for your dog's size, structure, and age. Even two dogs of the same breed, but with different angulations, may need different exercise plans. It is also a good idea to vary your exercise somewhat. If you do agility on Mondays, maybe do a hike on Tuesdays.

Poop Patrol

Think of poop patrol as a mission you need to accomplish. First, there is the basic need to clean up after your dog. That may mean a pooper scooper patrol in your fenced yard every couple of days or carrying baggies to pick up after your dog on walks and away from home. Hygiene is part of the mission. Along with keeping the yard safe to walk in and smelling fresh, you may also be helping to prevent zoonotic diseases. Both roundworms and hookworms can spread to people via dog fecal material.

So the first mission is clean yard, safe yard. Beyond simply picking up poop, it may also be important to inspect it. OK, you don't normally need a magnifying glass or a special cap like Sherlock Holmes, but it is important to check out your dog's stool now and then. Your dog could be having bouts of diarrhea but you never notice unless some gets caught on his tail feathers or he has an accident in the house. Families most often notice tapeworms when they go to pick up fresh poop and see white, rice-like segments moving around it.

Parasites and People

Roundworms, also known as ascarids, can infect people. Most commonly, young children are affected and can develop eye lesions from migrating parasites. Hookworms are less serious, but they can invade unbroken tissues and may be seen as linear sores picked up by going barefoot where dogs eliminated.

Changes in stool could mean a health problem. Taking a sample to your veterinarian—and no, you don't need a cup or more; a teaspoon will do—for a fecal flotation and microscopic exam can detect many parasites. Dogs should have a fecal check done at least once a year and more often if there are any problems or if your dog travels frequently.

Grooming: Squeaky Clean

Grooming is another important aspect of dog care. Just as you wouldn't dream of going out in public without brushing your hair, your dog's coat needs to be cared for, too. Removing dirt and other debris will help keep your dog's coat healthy, and routine grooming allows you to be aware of any lumps or sores on your dog's skin. This is important, because most health problems are less serious and easier to treat when caught quickly.

Depending on what breed your dog is, he may have different needs for coat care. Longhaired breeds like a Collie or a Shetland Sheepdog need almost daily grooming to keep their coats clean, whereas a Dalmatian is pretty much wash and wear. Some breeds, mostly hounds and terriers, have a stiff, wiry coat that needs to be hand stripped rather than brushed. Ask your veterinarian, groomer, or breeder for advice on the proper grooming of your dog.

There are many different types of brushes available for your dog. Slickers work well for a stiffer coat, while pin brushes work fine on a softer coat. If you have horses, a dandy brush works well on a dog with a short, tight coat such as a Dalmatian or a Greyhound. To help remove mats and snarls, there are also combs of every shape and size. Combs also work well for removing a rather stubborn undercoat.

Regular grooming will keep your dog clean most of the time, but on those rare occasions when your precious pooch covers himself in mud or rolls in something gross, he may need a bath. Dogs need baths only when they are dirty or before they go to a show. The exceptions are dogs with some types of skin problems; they may benefit from regular baths with medicated shampoos. In warm weather, you can use a

Grooming Essentials

Slicker: A brush with a rectangular head with small metal spikes; good for coated dogs and feathering.

Pin brush: A round brush with flexible metal pieces that stick up; excellent for long-coated dogs.

Mitt: A rubber glove that loosens up hair on short-coated dogs.

Comb: There are many; look for a Teflon one for the best results.

Scissors: Get a nice sharp pair to trim out mats and trim around feet.

Nail trimmers: These can be the guillotine type, scissor type, or a Dremel rotary tool.

backyard hose, but once winter sets in, you may have to use the bathtub. Be sure to use a dog shampoo that won't irritate his skin. To keep water out, put either cotton balls or a piece of tissue paper inside each of your dog's ears. Once clean, you can either let your dog run around to dry off or use a canine blow dryer. You can also use regular human hairdryers, but be aware that some of them produce heat, which could bother your dog.

No matter what type of dog you choose, there will be shedding. All dogs shed in the spring and fall to make the switch from their summer coat to their winter one or vice versa. You know that fall is coming when you wake up to drifts of hair floating around your kitchen! However, some breeds shed more than others, and some also shed year-round. Be sure to consult your breeder or veterinarian on this one, because a longhaired dog won't necessarily shed more than a shorthaired one. Our Pembroke Welsh Corgis shed far more than our Belgian Tervurens, who have much longer coats. Brushing your dog almost every day during the shedding season will help decrease the amount of hair in your house.

Grooming also includes the care of your dog's ears, eyes, nails, and teeth. Every now and then, check your dog's ears for any discharge or infection. Drop-eared dogs, especially dogs with long, heavy ears, such as Bassets and Cocker Spaniels, need to be checked frequently. If anything gets inside your dog's ear, try to remove it without hurting him. Redness, a bad smell, or any discharge could mean a problem such as ear mites or an infection. Your dog's eyes also need to be kept clean. If you notice foreign objects in your dog's eye, flush them out with artificial tears. This also works well for a dog with dry eyes. If your dog has a discharge or is squinting an eye, consider this an emergency and call your veterinarian.

Baloo is lying quietly for Kate to trim his nails.

Just like your fingernails, your dog's toenails need to be clipped just about once a week. As you can see in the photo, training your dog to lie down makes it easy to trim nails. You can use either special canine nail clippers or an electric rotary tool that files the nail down. Be careful not to clip his nails too short, because this could result in bleeding. White nails are easier to clip because you can see the end of the quick—the blood vessels and nerve endings in your dog's nail. Black nails are harder and require some guessing. If you do clip a nail too short, rubbing some soap onto the end of the nail will help stop the bleeding. A styptic pencil or silver nitrate stick will work, too. Don't panic at the sight of blood—as your dog walks around he can make a few drops look like a massacre! Be sure to start handling your dog's feet as soon as he enters your family—this will make toenail clipping much easier.

To prevent a buildup of tartar on your dog's teeth, you can brush them regularly or scale them (remember the pointed metal thing that your dental hygienist uses to scrape your teeth?). Dogs should use special toothpaste made for pets. Most human toothpastes are not designed to be swallowed. It can be very tricky to convince your dog to rinse and spit! Plus, dogs like the special pet flavors—most dogs prefer a chicken or some other meat-flavored toothpaste rather than mint or bubblegum. Most dogs don't mind having their teeth brushed, as you can see in the photo on page 58. You might want to keep your dog's toothpaste separate from your own—chicken toothpaste doesn't taste *that* good!

Dogs enjoy having their teeth brushed with flavored toothpastes.

Routine Care: What You Learned in Health Class

Preventive care is the buzzword in both human and veterinary health care. Using special medications to prevent flea and tick infestations (see chapter 6 for more on parasites), using vaccines as needed, and just observing your dog carefully can all be important parts of a preventive health care plan for your dog. Remember, *you* know your dog better than anyone else, so trust your intuition if you feel something is not right. Also, keep in mind that you are your dog's health care advocate.

The veterinary world, and the dog world in particular, is in the midst of deciding exactly what vaccines the average dog needs and how often. Vaccine manufacturers are testing vaccines for three-year durations, and veterinarians are looking at customized vaccine schedules for each dog. Your input will be valuable to your veterinarian as the two of you determine which vaccines and how often make sense for *your* individual dog.

You will see the words "core" and "non-core" bandied about in regards to vaccines. Core vaccines are vaccines that every dog should get. This is to safeguard their health from viruses that are present virtually everywhere. In the case of rabies, vaccination is required by law. Non-core vaccines are vaccines for diseases that may or may not be likely to cause your dog a problem. This covers diseases that aren't found everywhere and diseases that are usually treatable. Too many vaccines may overwhelm your dog's immune system, but not covering a serious disease could leave your dog at risk. You need to walk a fine line to determine what is necessary for your dog.

Core vaccines include

- Rabies
- Distemper
- Parvo
- Hepatitis/adenovirus

Non-core vaccines include

- Leptospirosis
- Bordetella
- Parainfluenza
- Giardia
- Corona
- Lyme

Virtually all states and many countries require your dog to have a rabies vaccine. This disease can spread from dogs to people and is almost always fatal. You don't want to skip this one. Puppies get one dose at 3 to 6 months of age, a booster at 1 year, and then usually every 3 years thereafter.

Distemper and parvo are viruses that are present almost everywhere. Dogs who get these viruses, especially as young dogs or puppies, have a high risk of dying, and if they survive may experience residual effects. Hepatitis/adenovirus is included in most combo vaccines, and it can also be fatal to dogs. Puppies and dogs of unknown vaccine history should have a series of two or three of these vaccines, a booster a year later, and then the frequency may vary with your dog's lifestyle.

In the non-core vaccines, Leptospirosis is becoming more of a problem in different areas of the United States. This spirchaete can cause fatal disease. Your veterinarian can let you know whether your dog is at risk in your area. Dogs who run in woods and fields or drink from ponds tend to have higher risk.

Bordetella and parainfluenza are associated with kennel or canine cough. These are not normally fatal diseases but can be serious in puppies. Many boarding facilities require this vaccine to help prevent the spread of respiratory problems. If one infected dog coughs in a building, the droplets can spread via the air to all the other dogs!

Giardia is a parasite that is mainly a problem in puppies and immune-suppressed dogs. Most dogs will not need this vaccine, as giardia infections can be treated with medications. Corona is a virus that causes diarrhea and intestinal upsets. Again, this is not normally a highly

For Parents Only

When it comes to routine care, your kids can certainly take responsibility for your dog. Feeding, exercising, and grooming can all be done by kids from fairly young on up. For very young kids, such as 4-year-olds, there should be close supervision; otherwise your spaniel could get a whole 10-pound bag of kibble for one meal. A young child can't be expected to always remember their duties, although if you establish a set routine it is easier. Luckily most dogs will remind you when it is time to eat!

If your dog needs some expert grooming help to detangle burrs or comb out feathering, your assistance may be needed. Trimming with scissors or using clippers should be done only under direct adult supervision. Still, most kids can do some basic grooming.

When it comes to exercise, make sure you pick something that will work for both child and dog. Having your 4-year-old daughter walk your adolescent male Lab down the street is probably not a great idea. However, that same kid/dog combo would be fine playing fetch with a ball in a fenced yard. Quite frankly, a family walk each evening with your dog is a nice way to end the day for everyone!

Although you do need to be on "standby" to help with crises and lend moral support, you also need to take a deep breath and take a step back. Learning to care for another living being is a wonderful step for your kids. They will develop empathy, patience, and responsibility. They will also at times experience frustration and upset. Despite some theories, a little adversity in childhood is not harmful to anyone's self-esteem, and the feeling of accomplishment when your child masters a difficult task like grooming your Collie is irreplaceable. So help, but don't overwhelm, and if you need to collapse in hysterical laughter, it might be better to go to another room.

serious disease. Your veterinarian will discuss with you whether your dog needs protection against this problem.

Lyme disease has been a regional problem but is spreading. This disease is spread via ticks. Your veterinarian will discuss with you where your dog goes and walks and whether tick prevention is adequate to keep this disease at bay or whether your dog would benefit from vaccination.

One of the most important parts of your dog's preventive health care plan is a frequent home physical exam. This can be done weekly or at least monthly. Most families do this while grooming the dog.

The plus here is that dogs have two of many body parts. Since dogs are normally symmetrical, you can compare one side to the other. If one ear has a discharge and the other is clean and light pink, you know one of them is not right. Gently running your hands over your dog's body, besides being a gentle massage, can make you aware of any lumps or bumps or differences in muscle mass. Any asymmetries should be further checked by your veterinarian.

In addition to your home physicals, your dog should have an annual (or even twice yearly if he is older) physical examination done by your veterinarian. This will include checking weight, looking down into ears, checking eyes carefully, and possibly routine blood work, plus a fecal sample evaluation. While this may seem expensive, catching problems early virtually always makes them easier to treat and less expensive in the long run.

Profile: Katelyn and Jake

Jake is known around our 4-H as "Big Jake"—and he is big, a large, neutered male German Shepherd Dog weighing almost as much as Katelyn. Still, when they started out together, Katelyn was bigger, and she has been firm but loving in her training of this big dog.

Katelyn was 14 years old when Jake came home to her family. He was just 8 weeks old, a small bundle of fuzz. Katelyn's dad was the one who was initially excited about adding a dog to the family, but Jake quickly became Katelyn's. While her dad occasionally helps with walking or feeding Jake, especially if Katelyn has school commitments, most of the care is done by her. So Katelyn grooms, bathes, feeds, exercises, and trains Jake almost all the time.

Katelyn feels that Jake has been an easy dog to train, even though he is her first dog. She says, "Training is a very slow and complex process. You have to start with the basics and practice often to be successful. When Jake was a puppy, the basics like Sit, Down, and Come came fairly easily, but I am still working on attention and heeling. The training and care never ends!" As with many young dogs (Jake is just 2 years old now), getting solid attention is difficult, especially in different surroundings and with other dogs around.

Jake and Katelyn have become a wonderful team in many areas. They compete in rally, grooming, handling (junior showmanship), obedience, and agility. As you can see in the photo on page 62, Katelyn and Jake have done well in junior showmanship. Jake has passed his CGC test with flying colors and is a certified Therapy Dog. Together Katelyn and Jake have been Reserve Grand Champion at the New York State Fair for two years in a row in agility! They are also in Open competition for junior showmanship at ASCA shows.

Katelyn and Jake are a top team in many areas.

One of Jake's favorite activities is playing Frisbee. He went through a rough spell with panosteitis, a growing-dog bone problem that resolves with time, but now he can run, jump, and play freely.

Katelyn feels Jake is special because "he is my friend and companion. He is always there whether I want him to be or not. He follows me around and is a great guardian of my secrets. I never thought that when we got him I would become this attached or even train him, as he is my first dog. He is everything I could have hoped for and then some. Yes, we have had some letdowns, but the feeling when we succeed as a team outweighs the setbacks." Jake has had problems doing rally—too many Sits, in his opinion!—and Katelyn had to delay some training due to his lameness problem. Still, they have persevered.

If you ask Katelyn what drawbacks there are to having a dog of her own, she is eloquent again. "It's a lot of work! It requires a lot of time. No matter how you feel, you have to get out in the snow and walk the dog. They need attention and care if they are sick. They are just like children; you have to watch over them to make sure they stay out of trouble and don't get hurt. Overall, the love and deep bond are well worth it."

We think this team has the whole human-animal relationship down pat!

6

Vet School: Dealing with Health Problems

Although we all hope that our dogs live long, healthy lives and never need to visit their veterinarian for reasons other than wellness visits, the reality is that most dogs will encounter some sort of health problem over their lifetimes. This could range from minor problems like parasites or a small wound to serious life-threatening illnesses such as bloat or cancer. This chapter is not intended as a shortcut to a DVM or VMD degree, but to make you aware of problems your dog might develop, how to help her, and when to contact your veterinarian.

ER—First Aid, Not the TV Show

The first rule of first aid is to stay calm. If you panic, your dog will panic, and it will be harder to help her. Don't worry if there is a little blood around—most people handle some blood just fine as long as they concentrate on taking care of the problem.

A second rule of thumb is to know *your* dog's normal values. Normal temperatures in dogs range from 100 to 102 degrees, give or take 0.5 degrees. Heart rates vary greatly with the size of the dog—from about 60 in a large dog to 150 or more in some small dogs. As you can see in the photo on page 64, you can check a pulse rate using the pulse in the groin area. Respiratory rates or numbers of breaths per minute run around 10 to 30.

Knowing Normals

To take your dog's temperature, use a rectal thermometer. Be sure to put some petroleum jelly on the tip before inserting so it slides easily. Heart rates can be counted by feeling your dog's heartbeat on her chest or reaching for the pulse in the groin area along the femur. Respiratory rate is determined by counting the number of breaths per minute.

One of the most common dog injuries is clipping a toenail too short. When this happens, there will be some blood. Although it may look like a lot of blood, this is just because your dog is walking around, spreading what might be just a few drops all over the floor—or the carpet, especially if the carpet is new and expensive. Again, remain calm. If you have a styptic pencil or a silver nitrate stick in the house—like the kind your dad uses after a shaving nick—put it right on the end of the nail. Although it will sting for a second, often just one application will stop the bleeding. Keep your dog quiet for a few minutes so that the blood can clot. Give her two cookies—one as an apology for cutting the nail too short and one for being good while you cauterized it. If you don't have a styptic pencil, push the nail into a bar of soap or a dish of cornstarch. Both methods help speed up clotting.

It is easy to feel the pulse in your dog's groin.

A cold-water hosing works well on acute lameness in a leg.

If your dog has a wound that is spurting or spraying bright red blood, an artery has been cut. You need to apply pressure directly to the area. Do not apply a tourniquet unless you are very skilled in first aid. A wound that seeps blood that is dark usually indicates damage to a vein. Again, apply pressure, but this type of wound will clot over more quickly. With either situation, if clotting does not occur quickly, you need to go to your veterinarian.

Acute lameness is very common in dogs. If your dog is out playing ball or catching a flying disc and suddenly comes up limping or holding a leg up, stop the game. If there is not an obvious broken bone, you can try simple first aid. The ideal immediate treatment is to run a hose with cold water over the injured leg for five minutes. Time this by your watch, as it can feel like forever, even when it has only been two minutes. As shown in the photo, the running water is cold but helpful. Then follow this up with an anti-inflammatory medication from your veterinarian or the proper dose of aspirin given with some food. Repeat in 12 hours and you will find that this takes care of many minor sprains and strains. Lameness that persists after a day needs some veterinary attention.

A dog in shock—whether from biting an electrical cord, heatstroke, or trauma—needs to be warmed up gently and taken to your veterinarian for fluids and steroids. Dogs in shock may shake, have very pale gums, and have rapid, shallow breathing.

Beware Electric Shocks!

If your dog has bitten into an electrical cord, unplug the cord or appliance before you go to touch the dog. It won't help your dog if you get shocked, too. If your dog is lying near downed wires, try to move her away from that area with a wooden stick or pole.

A dog who is choking or gagging and maybe even turning blue may have something stuck in her throat. *Very* carefully put your hand in your dog's mouth, and check to see if something is stuck in the back. You can use a wooden spoon or thick stick as a gag to prevent her from accidentally biting down on you. Try a modified Heimlich—squeezing her behind the ribs—to loosen up anything as well.

Heatstroke is fairly common, especially if you have an active dog and the weather is hot and humid. First, try to prevent heatstroke by monitoring your dog's activity, keeping her cool with shade and a fan, and having plenty of fresh, cool water for her to drink. If she does get overheated, you need to cool her down slowly. An ice pack in the groin area is helpful, and wiping paws with cool water is good, too. If she is disoriented, you need to get her to the veterinarian to be treated for shock.

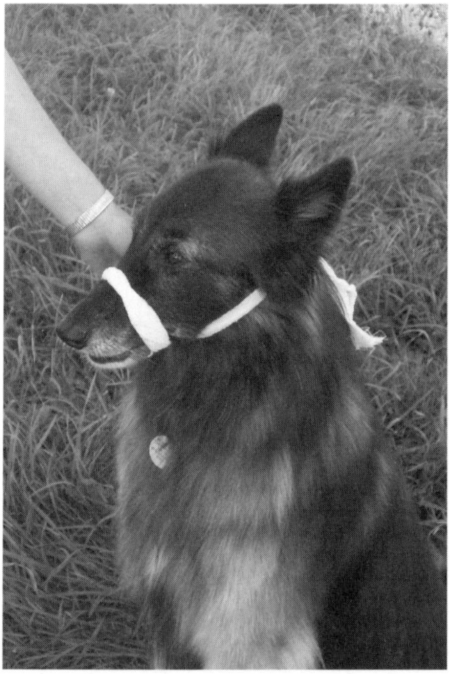

Applying a gauze muzzle is fairly quick and easy—you can't cut off your dog's breathing!

Even the sweetest, most loving dog might bite when she is injured and in pain. Therefore, it is important that you either own or know how to make a muzzle. You can use a sock, pantyhose, gauze, or even a tie to make an emergency muzzle. Simply make a loop in the material and slide it over your dog's nose. The photo shows Dani demonstrating a muzzle. Pull it tight and then tie a bow. Remember, your dog's nose has bone on the top and bone in the jaw underneath. You won't be cutting off her oxygen.

It is important to have a first-aid kit for your dog. Luckily, a first-aid kit for people contains many of the same things, so you can share one. A muzzle or muzzle-making material is one exception, even though you may think you would like one for some people you know! Bandaging material, ointments, and so on can be dual purpose.

Items for a Basic First-Aid Kit

- A roll of gauze for bandaging and making a muzzle
- Gauze pads
- Tape
- Scissors
- Antibiotic ointment
- Aloe or steroid ointment
- Antibacterial wash—chlorhexidine or betadine
- Artificial tears
- Aspirin
- Benadryl

Many Red Cross units offer both human and pet first-aid courses. Some even have a dog model for teaching CPR! These courses are usually inexpensive and very well taught. You can also ask your veterinarian or a local dog club about offering a first-aid class.

You can purchase ready-made first-aid kits or make your own very inexpensively by collecting the supplies at a discount store and putting them in a small plastic storage container. You may want to customize your kit by including emergency information about your pet and extras of any special medications your dog may need, such as an EpiPen if she is allergic to bee stings. Make sure that you get the proper dosage for any medications from your veterinarian and check expiration dates on medications regularly.

Dealing with Aliens—and This Isn't Science Fiction

Parasites are very much like aliens from another planet. If you don't think so, check out a close-up photo of a tapeworm, hookworm, tick, or flea. We are sure you will agree!

External Parasites

External parasites are tiny bugs that stay on the outside of your dog—usually making her itch, causing skin infections and hair loss, and in general, making her miserable. Some of them are contagious to you, too.

Fleas are extremely successful parasites. They are great athletes, able to run very fast and jump very high for their small size. You may notice brown blurs as you pull the hair aside near your dog's tail or see them run past the hairless area in her groin when she rolls over. Fleas can jump to your dog from other dogs, wildlife, or other pets. To get rid of fleas, you must not only kill the adult fleas, but also kill immature forms or larvae and eggs or prevent them from developing normally. Luckily, there are many new ways to fight fleas, including topical drops, flea growth inhibitor pills, and other standbys such as powders, sprays, dips, and shampoos.

Ticks are small, slow-moving parasites that hook into your dog's skin and stay in one spot for a bloodbath before dropping off. You may feel small, tense lumps that are grey/brown. These must be removed carefully to be sure you get the head and to keep any blood or fluids from getting on you.

Mites and lice can be harder to see, and some actually live in the outer layers of your dog's skin. If your dog is itching or has hair loss, your veterinarian may do a skin scraping to look for mites. Ear mites are small mites that build up dark, coffee ground–appearing wax in your dog's ears that may lead to infections and head shaking. Lice are often noticed due to their "nits" or immature forms glued to hairs.

External parasites can carry many diseases, some of which affect people, too. These diseases include Ehrlichia, tapeworms, Lyme disease, plague, and Rocky Mountain Spotted Fever. As with so many health problems, it is much easier to prevent parasite infestations than to treat them after they have become established. There are new topical medications that quickly kill or even repel ticks and fleas. Some of them work on mites and lice, too. You should talk to your veterinarian about the best parasite protection for your dog. And don't forget, if you plan to travel, let your veterinarian know that. We live in a low tick area but often travel to New England, which has a lot of ticks. Our dogs always get tick preventives before we head east.

Along with external parasites, we can include bugs such as deerflies, black flies, and bees. These aren't exactly parasites, as they can survive without your dog, but they can sting and bite your dog and make her miserable. Deerflies often bite the tips of prick-eared dogs' ears and leave sores that need daily care. Black flies can leave red or purple round sores in your dog's groin area. Bee stings hurt dogs just like they hurt us, and some dogs have allergic reactions just like some people.

Internal Parasites

Internal parasites use dogs—and sometimes people—as their hosts to provide them with nutrition and a safe haven. Of course, they don't ask permission first before moving in. Internal parasites include intestinal worms such as ascarids (roundworms), strongyles, hookworms, whipworms, and tapeworms.

You may see parasites in your puppy's stool or vomit if she has roundworms or as ricelike segments in the stool from tapeworms. Other internal parasites are detected by a microscopic exam of the stool by your veterinarian.

The photo shows models of adult worms. The bottom line is that these parasites drain needed nutrients from your dog, may cause diarrhea, and may cause disease in people, too, such as visceral larval roundworms in young children—sometimes leading to vision problems or even the loss of an eye. A puppy with a heavy infestation of roundworms or hookworms can even die. Doing a fecal check at least once yearly is important, and many heartworm preventives now include other parasite controls.

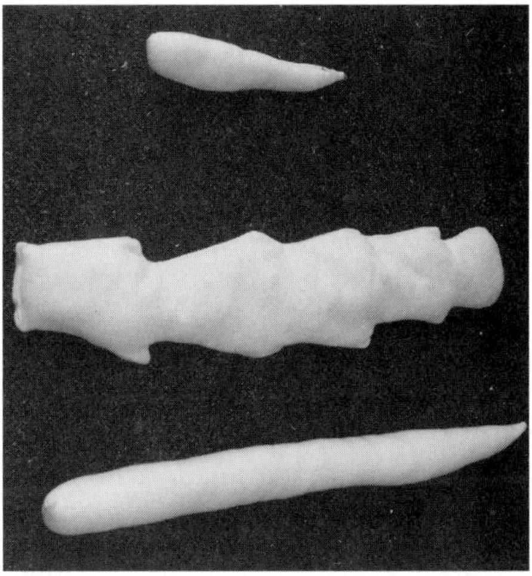

From top to bottom, these models show a hookworm, a tapeworm, and a roundworm.

Heartworm is an internal parasite that prefers to live in the heart and lungs of your dog. These parasites do damage to the heart and lungs and may be fatal. Dogs who have survived heartworms and heartworm treatment may have permanent damage to their heart, lungs, and liver. This is another case in which treatment is rougher and more expensive than prevention. After all, it is tricky to poison and kill off some of these parasites without causing any damage to your dog and her normal tissues. Most dogs do well on a monthly preventive medication.

Minor Illnesses

Just like people, dogs can have minor health problems or illnesses that you may even be able to treat at home. Some of these problems will require help from your veterinarian as well.

Arthritis

Arthritis may not be thought of as an illness, but it is a chronic condition that can cause your dog pain and even lead to euthanasia. Arthritis is inevitable in some dogs due to their conformation or structure. Other dogs are athletes who push their bodies to the limit and end up damaging joints. Genetics may play a part in the development of arthritis, too. Hip dysplasia is one of the best-known structural problems that can lead to arthritis.

Helpful ways for dealing with arthritis are to keep your dog fit and trim. Less weight means less stress on joints. Being fit means muscles can help do some of the work and keep joints moving. There are also nutritional supplements that seem to help keep joints healthy. These include chondroitin sulfate and glucosamine. Your veterinarian can help you with supplements that won't offset the balanced diet your dog is on. New research has shown

Sports Physicals

If your plans for your dog include a lot of athletic competitions such as agility, you should have her hips, elbows, and stifles checked by your veterinarian. The stifles—same as our knees—can be checked by careful palpation, but the hips and elbows will require sedation and radiographs or X-rays. These can be done at the same time as spaying or neutering.

that eicospentanoic acid, an omega-3 fatty acid, is also helpful for joint health.

Arthritic dogs do best with a moderate amount of exercise; walking and swimming can be excellent. These dogs should avoid jumping, twisting, and turning. Remember, the long daily walk is great for both of you! Our older Corgi, Susan, at 13½ years still enjoys her mile walk—maybe stroll is the better word—on the old railroad trail by our house.

Vomiting

Vomiting isn't pleasant for anyone—dogs included, although cats do seem to delight in vomiting up hairballs and parts of dead mice on your living room carpet. Still, repeated vomiting can lead to inhalation pneumonia, dehydration, and malnutrition. Many times dogs vomit because they ate something they shouldn't have. In this case, vomiting it back up is a good thing.

Still, if your dog is vomiting, you need to pay attention to the problem. She could be ill.

If your dog simply vomits up some phlegm, her stomach may just be a little upset. Yellow phlegm can mean bile. If there is bright red blood in the vomit, call your veterinarian.

Often, it will simply be your dog's food or the mouse she caught that morning. The first step is to see whether she can drink and keep water down. That way you know she won't become dehydrated. If she vomits up even clear water, you should call your veterinarian.

Grass Can Be Good

Dogs often eat grass just for salad, although they also use grass to help stimulate vomiting. Check out what type of grass your dog is wolfing down. Small, tender new grass is usually a salad choice. Longer, tougher grass is a vomiting stimulant.

If your dog can keep water down, offer her small amounts frequently. Meanwhile, no food for 24 hours. Don't give in to those begging eyes—stay tough! Just doing this will clear up many cases of mild stomach upset. After you start your dog back on food, use bland foods such as boiled chicken and rice. Feed small amounts frequently. If the vomiting continues or starts again, call your veterinarian.

Diarrhea

Diarrhea often accompanies vomiting but can occur alone. Even though it seems gross, you need to look at the diarrhea and save some to take to your veterinarian. If there is blood in it, your dog could have certain parasites or damage to her intestinal wall. By looking at the diarrhea under a microscope, your veterinarian can search for parasites or their eggs.

One of the best treatments to do at home is not to feed your dog for 24 hours. Make sure that she has plenty of water so that she won't get dehydrated, but no food. Just letting the stomach and intestines have a rest can be very helpful. Certainly if diarrhea lasts more than a day, you need to call your veterinarian. After the diarrhea has stopped, go on to the bland chicken and rice diet for a day or so and gradually work back to her normal diet.

Two of the few exceptions for going 24 hours without food are diabetic dogs and Toy breed puppies who may have blood sugar problems if they fast. In these cases, call your veterinarian for guidance.

Sneezing and Coughing

Dogs may sneeze or cough occasionally just like we do. If your dog is coughing frequently, has a discharge, and can't exercise as much as usual, she needs to be checked by your veterinarian. A cough could mean anything from a mild virus—like our common cold—to something serious such as pneumonia or heartworm. Heart problems may first show up as a cough, too. If your dog is coughing, she should avoid going to any dog classes or shows, because you don't want her to spread a respiratory virus. This is the same as you staying home from school when you have a bad cough.

Hair Loss

Hair loss combined with less activity and weight gain may indicate a hormonal problem. The most common hormonal problem in dogs is low thyroid levels. This problem can be diagnosed with a blood test, and your dog may need to take thyroid medication. Luckily, the medication is not very expensive. Hair loss can also come from a poor diet, parasites, or a skin infection. If your dog's hair loss is more than normal shedding, she may need to see a veterinarian.

More Serious Health Problems

Along with minor ailments, dogs can also have serious health problems. Many of these are the same as human health problems, and dogs may even be prescribed the same medications. Do not share medications with your dog, though, as the doses are often very different in amount and/or frequency.

Bloating

Bloat (or gastrointestinal dilatation/volvulus—see, don't you like "bloat" better?) is when your dog has an accumulation of gas and (usually) undigested food in her stomach. The swelling may be visible from the outside, and she may try to vomit but nothing comes up. The stomach may actually twist and shut off the blood flow to it, which is a very serious complication. If you suspect bloat, head for your veterinarian right away.

Cancer

Cancer is one of the most dreaded words in our language. Although many dogs, especially older ones, experience cancer, it doesn't have to be a death sentence. Cancers come in a wide range of types, some of which are more serious than others. Surgery, radiation, chemotherapy, and diet adjustments may all be included in your dog's treatment. Don't hesitate to consult a veterinary oncologist if your dog is diagnosed with a serious cancer.

Cancer Types

There are many kinds of cancer in dogs. Some are benign, like histiocytomas, which are small, red tumors that are often seen on young dogs. Surgery is curative. Other cancers, such as osteosarcoma or bone cancer, are very malignant and aggressive. Pain medications are an important part of treating cancer patients.

Car Accidents

The most common cause of trauma in dogs is being hit by a car. The use of a leash could prevent almost all of these accidents. If your dog escapes your fenced yard or darts out a door—remember the wait-at-doors training?—immediately go to search for her. If you spot her and she doesn't come when called, try running in the opposite direction or lie down and pretend to be fascinated by something on the ground. Either way, many dogs will come over to investigate with you, as they are very nosy.

Still, accidents *do* happen, and if your dog is hit, you need to respond right away. If there is blood spurting, put pressure on it. Make sure she is breathing. See whether she is responsive and aware. Be prepared to tie a makeshift muzzle on her in case she is hurting and could bite out of pain. Look for any obvious broken bones. If she is unable to move, bring a

Eye Problems

If your dog is suddenly squinting an eye, flush it gently with artificial tears. Dust, seeds, and pollen can all irritate your dog's cornea just like they can irritate your eye. Often these irritants will scrape or injure the cornea. Your dog may need medication to heal the eye without leaving a scar.

blanket or board to gently slide her onto. You will need help for most of this, so don't hesitate to ask someone. Have someone else drive to the veterinarian while you keep your dog calm.

Eye Problems

Any change in your dog's eyes is a reason to call your veterinarian. Eye problems can go from minor and treatable to very serious in very little time. Redness, squinting, and any discharge are all reasons to check in with your veterinarian. Immediately flushing the eye with artificial tears is a good idea.

Liver, Heart, and Kidney Problems

Liver, heart, and kidney problems are other older-dog health problems. Although young dogs may develop these problems, they are more common in seniors. These are often problems that cannot be totally cured, but many of them can be controlled or managed to give your dog a reasonable quality of life. Diet and medication are often involved in their treatment.

Seizures or Epilepsy

Seizures or epilepsy are seen in a wide range of dog breeds and mixed breeds. If your dog goes into a seizure, *do not* worry about her swallowing her tongue! It simply can't be done, and instead, many people end up going to the emergency room themselves when their dog unconsciously bites them. Simply try to keep your dog calm, make sure she can't fall down stairs or bang her head badly, and wait it out. Most seizures end in a minute or less, although it feels like forever to you. If the seizures last longer than three to five minutes, you need to head to your veterinarian. After the actual seizure ends, your dog may be somewhat disoriented. She may have peed or pooped while seizing, but she couldn't help it. Keep her quiet and let her rest, because seizures are very energy consuming.

There are many causes for seizures, but genetic epilepsy is one of the most common. Your veterinarian will take a careful history and do blood work and other tests to rule out poisons, cancer, and other causes. Seizures can be treated with medications, both to stop the seizure itself and to prevent future ones.

Other Ailments

Some problems have known genetic connections. If your dog is a purebred and you know that some dogs of that breed have certain problems, be aware of them. It might mean doing yearly eye checks or frequent urine sample checks. You want to be on top of any problems and catch them early when treatment is most effective.

Euthanasia

One of the worst realities of having a dog as a family member is knowing that her lifespan will be shorter than yours. Still, we have the privilege of removing all pain and discomfort when we can no longer keep our dogs comfortable. Euthanasia actually means "good death" in Greek, and that is the goal of your veterinarian working with you.

Your dog may receive a sedative first and may need a catheter put in if her veins are old or not working well. Then an injection is given in the vein that shuts down her heart, brain, and lungs. Right away you notice the loss of the blink reflex, showing that the brain is gone. The heart and lungs stop next. Ideally this goes quickly and virtually painlessly.

How do you know when it is time to euthanize your dog? It should never be for convenience—such as you want a new carpet or you want a new puppy. Instead, you should look at the quality of life your dog has. Sometimes your dog will convey that it is time herself, and you will just "know" it is time.

In examining her quality of life, ask the following questions:

- Does she have more good days than bad days?
- Can you control her pain, or is she in discomfort?
- Can she eat, drink, and eliminate?
- Can she do the things she loves to do most?

When you realize the time is drawing near, try to spend some extra time with your dear buddy. Sitting quietly, petting her, talking to her, and letting her know just how much you love her is important for both of you. The decision to euthanize your beloved friend is one of the most difficult and unselfish decisions you will ever make when it

For Parents Only

Having a dog does mean having to deal with some health problems and health-related expenses. It is best to be upfront with your children about expenses and what your family can afford. Most veterinary clinics will try to work out payment arrangements with you. Some families keep a separate credit card just for unexpected expenses that could include veterinary bills.

Don't underestimate your kids! You may be surprised at the creative ideas they come up with to help out with bills for a beloved dog who needs surgery. Kids are also often outstanding nurses and caretakers for injured, wounded, or sick dogs.

Remember that your dog *is* a family member. Treat her with love and respect and help preserve her dignity as she ages. Our elderly Corgi is quite deaf, and it can be frustrating when we call to her from 10 feet away and she can't hear us, or when she needs help going up the three steps in front of the house. Still, it is worth it to us just to enjoy her sunny face and the way she looks at us with love—especially if we have food!

When it comes time for euthanasia, be honest with your children. Otherwise, they seem to feel something sneaky and underhanded was done. Most kids realize deep down when it is time, perhaps better than we adults do. If you have any feelings about an afterlife, I think you can feel certain that your beloved dogs will be there waiting for you. I know I expect to see all of my beloved companions.

is made out of love. There are many good books that can help you through this time (see Appendix A).

Plan a memorial ceremony. You may want to collect some of her hair or make a paw print cast. Donations made in your dog's memory to an animal shelter can help ease not only *your* sorrow, but also the pain of some other dog.

Dealing with the death of your dog is very, very hard. You may want to bury her at home if you have a suitable place. There are pet cemeteries that provide perpetual care. You may also choose cremation and ask for ashes to keep. No solution is perfect, but do what feels right for you.

Profile: Becky and Vicky

Becky was just 6 years old when she picked out Vicky. Despite having a room full of cute Shetland Sheepdog puppies in front of her, Becky chose the slightly older bitch—Vicky was not quite a year old yet. Unfortunately, Vicky was just a couple of years old when she was diagnosed with lupus and arthritis. Becky chose to keep Vicky with the goal of simply keeping her comfortable. The breeder offered her another pup to work with as well, and Robbie joined their family when Becky was 9 years old. Robbie was only 10 weeks old, but Becky was now old enough to take over much more of the little puppy's care.

In Becky's family, everyone helped with mealtimes, especially if Becky had school commitments. Still, she was expected to do the grooming and general care, including exercising and training, for her Shelties.

"Both Shelties were typical herding dogs and loved to work and learn new things," according to Becky. Becky feels Robbie even learned the tough "drop on recall" by watching Becky's mom work her own dog!

Despite Becky's young age when she got Vicky, Vicky picked up on things quickly. She was very smart and did 4-H, obedience, and herding with Becky. Her illness forced her retirement, but she was a beloved family member for many years, even though her initial prognosis was poor.

Robbie and Becky had a special bond.

Robbie was also a quick learner. He would follow the other dogs and pick up pointers. The basics such as Sit, Down, Come, and Heel were all very easy for him to learn. Clicker training was trickier. Becky says, "Robbie would offer behaviors so quickly that I could not always 'capture' or mark the behavior I wanted. When I was trying to teach him to spin in a circle, he ended up with this funny behavior where he would turn his head and back up. He looked so funny and I couldn't get past that, so we had to abandon the spin idea." With Robbie, Becky branched out into junior showmanship and agility as well as doing obedience and 4-H.

Vicky was very special to Becky because she was her very first dog. She also was a fighter despite her disease. At the time of her diagnosis of lupus, the veterinarians predicted that she would not live much longer. Vicky however, had other ideas. She lived to be 11 and stayed quite active up to the end. As she got older, her arthritis became more obvious, but she still remained spry. "One night when Vicky was older and quite arthritic, we mistakenly left the leftover pizza on the dining room table. Vicky managed to get up on the table and eat the pizza without pulling the tablecloth and with all the chairs pushed in! To this day we have no idea how she did it."

Robbie had 12 special years with Becky. He was a dog who got frightened easily when he was young but quickly learned to trust Becky. "He trusted me so much that he would do anything I asked him because he knew I wouldn't do anything to hurt him," says Becky. Clearly the strong bond goes both ways. As you can see in the photo on page 76, Becky and Robbie truly enjoyed one another's company.

Becky doesn't feel there are any drawbacks to having a dog of your own. "When you have your own dog, you have a friend for life. They are always there when you need them. In showing dogs, you have a fun hobby that can last throughout your own lifetime."

Unfortunately, Becky has had to face the loss of both her special dogs. "When Vicky passed on, we had known for years that it was coming. We had her entire life to face that someday she would be gone. Toward the end of her life, it was apparent she was having problems, so I could start to cope with it. With Vicky, every day was a gift, because she wasn't supposed to live as long as she did. It was still difficult to make that final decision, though."

While Becky was prepared for Vicky's demise, Robbie was still a bouncy 12-year-old when he died. He had had some growths that recurred and went in for exploratory surgery. Sadly, he passed away while under anesthesia. As Becky says, "There was no warning. One day he was a basically healthy dog, and the next he was gone. Losing an animal is always a terribly hard thing to deal with. They are our companions, our friends, and a part of the family."

Becky is now in law school and can't have a dog. She is hoping to find just the right Sheltie to join her life when she graduates and heads out to face the world. After all, everybody can use a friend who is there for you 24/7.

7

Going for a PhD in Obedience

Many different competitions are available for you and your dog to show off everything he can do. Remember the commands Sit, Down, Stand, Come, and Stay that you taught your dog for use around the house? Obedience competitions test your dog's ability to do all these things and more as close to perfect as possible in a strange place.

Where to Train

The first step to take toward competing in obedience is to sign up for a class. The best way to find a good class is to contact your local dog club and find out what classes they have available and when. Most classes are six to eight weeks long with sessions once a week for thirty to sixty minutes. Another option is looking into private trainers in your area. These are often experienced competitors who may offer private or group lessons. Follow the same criteria as for lessons from a club.

Before signing up, you should consider a few things. The facility is a very important factor. You want to make sure that it is safe and comfortable for you and your dog. If you are taking classes during the winter, keep in mind that you may not want to drive two hours each way at night, and try to find a route to the facility that uses main roads that will be plowed frequently. If the class is in the city, be sure that you feel comfortable in that area and search for grass where you can walk your dog.

Also look into footing and doorways. Make sure the floor isn't slippery or in any way potentially dangerous for you or your dog. For doorways, figure out the system—some facilities have one "in" door and one "out" door, and others have multiple side doors that people can use depending on where they park. We used to train in part of a shopping mall, and the doors were motion activated. Thus, there were often gates by the doors to prevent dogs from escaping. And even more important, make sure that the facility and the club that offers the classes are kid and family friendly. There is no point in taking classes if you are just going to be looked down upon because you are a kid.

Health concerns are important, too. Most training facilities want proof of health care and vaccinations as well as fecal checks. Remember, this is for the good of your dog. You don't want your dog exposed to sick or parasite-laden pets.

After you've found a facility that you are comfortable with and that has the right class for you and your dog, you might want to pay a visit just to watch how the classes are run. You want to make sure that the instructor you might be taking classes from does not intimidate you. A good class has people busy, and obviously both the people and their dogs are having fun. The class should appear to be under control, but relaxed. Remember, training and doing obedience is, and should be, fun for both you and your dog.

It is also a good idea to make yourself familiar with the class format. Some instructors like to talk at the beginning of each class, and others prefer to discuss things as they occur. If you are a hands-on kind of person, don't take classes from a lecturer. See what types of dogs and people are in the classes—you can learn a lot about the instructor just from observing the

The Ideal Training Center

You want to be sure both you and your dog are comfortable in your training classes. There are some specific factors you should consider when looking for a training facility. These include:

- A friendly, helpful instructor
- Students and their dogs successful and having fun
- A safe facility
- A convenient location
- Reasonable costs

students. Some classes may be made up entirely of experienced-looking handlers, and others consist of beginners who are just being introduced to the dog world. Also observe the type and size of the dogs, as some instructors may specialize in little dogs, while others may focus on difficult or problem dogs.

If you decide not to take classes, you can train on your own, although this can be difficult for a beginner. If you do make this decision, don't fall into the trap of working your dog only at home. Most pet stores allow dogs to come in, and they provide excellent distractions—especially the open treat bins! The local dog training facility will probably offer open training nights when you can work your dog on your own for a few dollars.

There are many good training books you can read with your dog.

If you decide to train on your own, there are many good books and videos that can guide you along, as well as dog obedience magazines. As the photo shows, your dog will want to read with you! Many of the top trainers also have Web sites that offer training tips and articles. Seminars with top trainers can also be very helpful. It is also nice if you can find a training partner to work with. A simple notice on a bulletin board may give you a new friend to work with. Having a training partner or going to class helps you stay dedicated to working your dog.

Some people find it most convenient to schedule a private lesson with a top trainer once a month and train on their own in between. This works very well if the trainer you truly admire lives a distance away. You might even find a carpool partner to travel with!

Maintaining Consistency

Don't try to switch your entire training program abruptly after attending a seminar or watching a great video. Expect to get one to three top tips from a seminar—sometimes about what not to do!—and slowly incorporate these things into your program. Otherwise, your poor dog gets semi-trained and very confused with the "method of the week."

Basic Levels

Different venues often have slightly different rules and levels, but there are four basic levels of competition that almost all venues use, although some have even more.

You will hear dog people talk about earning "titles" or "legs." A title is a set of letters added to your dog's name after he has successfully competed at least three times under multiple judges. Each successful pass is called a leg. So your dog needs three *legs* to earn a *title*.

Pre-Novice

The bottom level of the pyramid is Pre-Novice. In most venues, this is a non-titling class that is offered just for handlers with young dogs who aren't ready for the upper levels. This consists of a heel on-leash exercise, figure 8 (heel a figure 8 around either two cones or people), stand for exam (dog is left in a stand stay while a judge runs hands over his back), recall or coming when called, one-minute Sit Stay, and three-minute Down Stay. Everything is on leash. As you can see in the photo, a heeling dog walks on your left side on a loose leash.

This lovely English Springer Spaniel shows nice heeling form.

Novice

Novice is the first titling level. To earn your title, you and your dog must earn qualifying scores three times under at least two different judges. This class consists of a heel on-leash exercise, figure 8, stand for exam, heel off leash, recall, one-minute Sit Stay, and three-minute Down Stay. The heel on leash and figure 8 are the only exercises done on leash. Dogs at this level have done very well in basic obedience and manners.

Heeling

Heeling is an exercise in which your dog must walk along your left side, matching any changes of pace you do, not pulling on the leash, and sitting automatically whenever you stop. A beautiful heeling dog is like a good dance partner.

Types of Matches

Matches are practice for the real thing—like scrimmages your soccer team plays before a real game against another school. There are different types of matches:

- **Fun Match:** A practice show where food, clickers, and toys are usually allowed, but if you are going for awards you may not use them. Ribbons and prizes are awarded.
- **Sanctioned Match:** This is truly a practice show. The rules for real shows are observed, but you can't earn legs toward your titles. Ribbons and prizes are awarded.
- **Show 'n Go:** This is strictly practice *runs*—chances to have your dog do the show routine. No ribbons or prizes are awarded.
- **FEO:** For exhibition only—this means that you are working your dog at the match but are not eligible for prizes.

Open

The second titling level is Open. This is a more difficult class and requires a lot more training. Your dog must be able to perform the heel off leash, figure 8, drop on recall (call your dog and, when the judge gives you the signal, either signal or tell your dog to lie down), retrieve on the flat (throw a plastic or wooden dumbbell for your dog to retrieve), retrieve over the high jump (this time you throw the dumbbell over a jump and your dog has to jump it both on the way out and back), broad jump (you stand beside a wide, low jump and have your dog jump over it and come to the front), three-minute Sit Stay, and five-minute Down Stay. The photo shows a dog at the Open level with her dumbbell. The entire class is off leash, and the stays are out of sight. Dogs really enjoy Open as they get to fetch and jump.

Dani clearly shows a good Hold with her dumbbell.

Utility

Utility is the third and final level. Dogs in utility are like PhD candidates. They are working on some difficult exercises. These dogs are off leash the entire class and must work with just hand signals part of the time, do scent discrimination,

follow directions to retrieve one of multiple items, stand reliably for exam, and run out to set themselves up for a directed jumping exercise. It's lots of fun, but lots of work is necessary to reach this level.

Note that official competitions that lead to titles, or letters you can put behind or in front of your dog's registered name are called shows or trials. These are run by strict guidelines of the organization sponsoring them, and only registered dogs may compete. At real trials, you are not usually allowed to carry food, toys, or a clicker in the ring. Matches are practice shows. They provide practice for you before you pay the higher entry fees at a real show and provide practice for the club members in running a show.

Some other shows also offer Brace, Team, and Graduate Novice. Like Pre-Novice, these are all nontitling.

Brace

Brace requires two dogs—usually attached by a coupler, which may remain on at all times or can be removed. Some people simply use two separate leashes instead. This class is run just like Novice with all the same requirements.

Team

Team consists of four dog-and-handler teams working together. This class has the same exercises as Novice, except for the recall. The recall is a Drop, like in Open. Scoring includes how well synchronized your team is as well as how every dog performs each exercise.

Graduate Novice

Graduate Novice is the halfway point between Novice and Open. The exercises are heel on leash, figure 8, drop on recall, dumbbell recall (the dog is left on a Stay with the dumbbell in his mouth and comes to the front when called—just like a regular recall but with the dumbbell in the dog's mouth), recall over high jump (the dog is left on Stay and then called over the high jump), recall over broad jump, and three-minute Down Stay out of sight. This is the rarest of the non-regular classes.

Competitive Venues

After you have started taking classes, you might want to look into what venues you eventually would like to compete in. Many different clubs and organizations offer titling competitions for registered dogs. There are options for All American dogs as well.

Before you think about entering a competition, you need to be sure your dog is *proofed*. Although this sounds like whiskey testing, it is totally nonalcoholic.

Your dog needs to be proofed to ignore distractions such as toys.

Proofing means that your dog understands he must come to you even if a person standing by the ring is eating a hot dog. The photo shows a dog being proofed to ignore toys. Proofing means that your dog must come when you call him, even if he is in a group of playing dogs. There are an endless number of distractions you can proof for, but we tend to stick to realistic ones like food, toys, and other dogs.

4-H

Joining 4-H is a good choice for kids between the ages of 9 and 18. 4-H is for kids only and accepts all breeds and mixes. To get started, go to your local Cooperative Extension and ask to sign up for dog 4-H. You can then either track down and join a club in your county or train on your own as an individual. Most clubs have weekly training sessions with an experienced trainer. This is a great opportunity to teach your dog new things, learn more about the sport, and make new friends. In the spring or summer, all the dog 4-H kids in your county will get together and have a competition. These shows usually offer obedience, as well as some other sports that you will learn about later. The top three kids from each level then go on to compete at a statewide competition with other counties.

Dog 4-H obedience has seven levels in all, and each is divided into A and B. A is for those who have never competed at that level before, and B is for those who have. The first level is Beginner, which is the equivalent of Pre-Novice. Next is Graduate Beginner, which is almost the same as Novice but doesn't have a heel off leash. Therefore, the stand for exam, recall, and stays are the only things off leash. Novice is next, followed by Graduate Novice and Pre-Open. Not all 4-H programs offer these classes, and the requirements may vary. Basically, these classes are to help with the transition from Novice to Open, and you should contact your Cooperative Extension to find out the exact specifications for your state. The last two levels are Open and Utility. 4-H also offers three extra classes that are just for fun. These are Brace, where each handler has two dogs attached by a coupler; four-person team, which consists of four people trying to do everything together and precisely; and Drill team, which requires a minimum of eight people and dogs doing obedience work and other related moves to music for a specific amount of time.

4-H uses the Danish system, in which everyone gets a ribbon. The ribbons come in three colors, each of which represent a range of scoring. Blue is for Excellent, Red is for Good, and White is for Worthy.

AKC

Whereas 4-H is a non-titling organization, there are others that are. The American Kennel Club (AKC) is for purebred registered dogs only, although if you have a spayed or neutered dog who looks like a purebred, but you don't have papers, you can get him an Indefinite Listing Privilege (ILP) number that will allow him to compete in every AKC sport except conformation. AKC is the most readily available titling organization, with shows every weekend across the United States. The obedience classes are Novice, Open, and Utility, although some shows also offer the non-titling classes Pre-Novice, Brace, Team, and Graduate Novice. AKC has a junior recognition program for any junior handler at least 9 years old and not yet 18. Every time you earn a qualifying score, fill out a Junior Handler form and turn in the bottom copy to the superintendent. After your dog earns his title, you will receive a certificate stating that you, a junior handler, showed your dog to whatever title you earned. You will also receive a pin with an attachment that has the title on it.

Competition Obedience

Training for competition means more precision and perhaps some exercises your pet dog wouldn't need. There are many excellent trainers, books, and videos that concentrate on training for competition. Plus, seminars are offered around the country by top trainers. Check out Appendix A for more information.

The Canadian Kennel Club offers classes very similar to the American Kennel Club. Many exhibitors who live near the border cross over to earn titles on both sides.

UKC

The United Kennel Club (UKC) is another organization that offers obedience titles. UKC allows not only registered dogs to compete in their performance

events but also mixed breeds. All mixes and dogs without a three-generation pedigree are given Limited Privilege registration numbers. These dogs can do anything except conformation and must be spayed or neutered. UKC offers titles in Novice, Open, and Utility. Sub-Novice (the equivalent of Pre-Novice), Graduate Novice, Graduate Open, and Team are also offered at some shows as non-regular classes. All UKC obedience trials are required to offer High Scoring Junior Handler. Any junior handler age 8–18 can compete for this award, and every time you compete in obedience you will earn five points toward the annual Top Ten competition. Placements earn additional points.

ASCA

The Australian Shepherd Club of America (ASCA) is another excellent organization to be involved in. All breeds and mixes can compete in anything except conformation, which is for Australian Shepherds only. Titles are offered in Novice, Open, and Utility, all of which go by the same rules as the AKC. Most ASCA shows also offer Sub-Novice (the equivalent of Pre-Novice) and Brace. Every show offers High Scoring Junior Handler. ASCA is an extremely user-friendly organization and great for kids.

Rally Obedience

Rally obedience is taking the dog world by storm. This is a sport that combines elements of agility and obedience. Your dog will need to complete a numbered course with you—following the numbers in order and performing exercises printed out on signs. It is also timed. Low jumps are included at the upper levels, and even in the lower level you have fun things like spirals and serpentines. The first level is on leash, and then you have to go off leash. Dogs are judged on their performance of the exercises, although the judging is not as precise as in regular obedience. Plus, handlers are allowed to talk more, pat their legs, make silly noises, and so on. Dogs really think this is fun!

This table shows the different levels and titles of obedience and rally in AKC with the letters that would then be added to your dog's name. Flash is a CD RAE titled dog, meaning she has a Companion Dog obedience title and a Rally Advanced Excellent title.

Level	Title
Novice	Companion Dog CD
Open	Companion Dog Excellent CDX
Utility	Utility Dog UD

continued

Level	Title
Open B *and* Utility B	Utility Dog Excellent UDX
Open B *and* Utility B	Obedience Trial Champion OTCH
Novice Rally	Rally Novice RN
Advanced Rally	Rally Advanced RA
Excellent Rally	Rally Excellent RE
Advanced B *and* Excellent B Rally	Rally Advanced Excellent RAE

Rally courses can be a challenge for handlers. You need to be able to walk, read the signs, and keep track of your dog all at once—sort of like walking and chewing gum! You do get to walk the course without your dog first as a group at the beginning of the class. This way you are familiar with the signs and where to go. Signs will tell you where and how to turn, but the

In advanced rally, the dog must jump as the handler runs with him.

For Parents Only

At first, obedience and rally may seem to be way over the heads of your kids and their dogs. However, you will quickly find that with positive instructors, kids and dogs will zoom along. Very often kids don't have the worries we adults do—they often simply assume that they and their dogs can do anything. Add in a little sweat and effort and they are often right. One of the best things about obedience and rally is that *any* dog can do these sports. Old dogs, young dogs, couch potato dogs, wild teenage dogs who need some focus and structure—all of these dogs can do obedience and rally.

Likewise, if you have a child who is not a super athlete and gets overwhelmed just looking at an agility course, here is a chance for her to shine. If you are a one-dog family with more than one child who wants to train, you can split the sports—letting one child do rally, another obedience, and so on.

If you have a child who needs to work on reading, rally signs are an easy way to practice. Spatial orientation, following directions, and learning good habits about daily practice are all part of working with your dog in obedience and rally. The bonds formed between a working dog and his partners are incredibly strong. After you have experienced it, I guarantee you will train every dog you live with after that—even if you decide to forgo actual competitions.

Obedience can be incredibly fun to share, too. When your dog knows how to retrieve or do scent discrimination, he will be a hit at demos, school visits, nursing home visits, and so on. Our dogs have done hand signals and retrieving for kids with special needs and as rewards for kids who are being tutored. Dogs, at least well-trained, well-behaved dogs, make friends wherever they go!

walk-through makes you feel more comfortable. Jumps get added to the two advanced levels but aren't seen at the Novice level. Your footwork can be very important in rally, so be sure you understand the signs exactly.

Since rally does incorporate many basic obedience moves and exercises, it can be an excellent way to start off your young dog in obedience events. Retired dogs think it is fun, too, and dogs who are working up to the next level of obedience competition may enjoy it as a break. All six of our dogs competed at the first AKC rally trials and all earned titles—from the 7-month-old Belgian Tervuren to the almost 13-year-old Pembroke Welsh Corgi!

APDT or Association of Pet Dog Trainers was the first group to work out rally. Following the ideas of Bud Kramer, they have developed three levels of rally plus championships. They do allow you to carry food during a run, but it can be used only as a reward after stationary exercises—for example, you can't lure your dog around with a hot dog! APDT stresses positive training, and their courses are longer and more difficult at the beginner level than the AKC's. Following their association's credo, all dogs are eligible to do APDT rally, even mixed breeds and dogs with handicaps. APDT rally titles are Level 1, Level 2, and Level 3. Level 1 is done on leash; the upper levels are done off leash and include more exercises, some of which are more difficult.

The American Kennel Club now offers rally as well, and the United Kennel Club and Australian Shepherd Club of America may both offer it in the future. AKC rally has three levels, plus you can continue to compete in both top levels for an advanced title. AKC does not allow food, toys, or clickers in the ring, but you can talk to and encourage your dog and pat your leg at the lower levels. Time is used to break any ties in AKC competitions. AKC levels are Novice, Advanced, and Excellent. Novice is totally on leash, while the upper levels are off leash and include jumps and some tougher exercises such as pivots.

Some rally signs include

- **Halt, Sit, Walk around Dog**
- **270 Right:** These make you remember your math!
- **Spiral Dog on Outside:** This is a paperclip-shaped course around cones.
- **Call Front, Finish Right:** Your dog must come and sit in front, and then return to heel position at your left side by going around you.

Along with doing serious rally for titles, you can have a lot of fun with this concept. We have made up some of our own rally signs, incorporating freestyle moves and fun things. Signs might say "Sit Dog, Handler Sing Happy Birthday" or "Dog Spins at Handler's Side." We should warn you—most rally courses have plenty of spins and circles. You may find that you get dizzy even if your dog doesn't!

Many clubs now offer rally classes, and there are some excellent books on the subject. It is important to learn the signs and practice the individual exercises. Many families print out their own signs to laminate and practice with.

Profile: Brie and Blaze

Brie started working with dogs when she was 7 years old but didn't get a dog of her own until she was 12. At age 12, she got her blue merle Shetland Sheepdog, Blaze. Brie had researched breeds and decided Australian Shepherds and Shetland Sheepdogs were two breeds she liked. Since her family already had two big dogs (a Labrador Retriever and a Rottweiler), the smaller breed seemed to be the way to go.

Brie researched breeders and found a great one. To pay for her pup, Brie worked for the breeder, and a year after her search started, she had a beautiful blue merle boy, Blaze! She now has two more Shelties, Buzz and Gwen. Buzz and Gwen were rehomes—in Buzz's case, the breeder simply did not need another male dog, and in Gwen's case, her owner had problems and had to return her at a year and a half of age. Both were welcome additions to Brie's household.

Brie and Blaze are a dynamic duo in performance.

Blaze was 9 weeks old when Brie got him. Even as a little puppy, Blaze was extremely clever and loved to learn new things. When he was 6 months old, Brie showed him in Beginner at the New York State Fair, earning Reserve Grand Champion! He can learn a new trick in ten minutes flat and prefers to do many different things for short amounts of time rather than spend a whole fifteen minutes on one exercise or trick.

Right from the start, Brie took over most of his care. She feeds, grooms, bathes, walks, cleans up after, and trains all three of her Shelties and wouldn't have it any other way. The bond she has with her dogs is evident as soon as you meet her. As you can see in the photo, they are a true working team!

Brie says that Blaze is special because he was the first dog who was totally hers and always seems to know what she expects of him. Heeling was the easiest thing to train, although she adds that the automatic sits on halts were a bit of a trial. Blaze is very active, and staying still is not easy for him. Now that Brie and Blaze have earned their Open obedience titles, they are getting ready for Utility. Scent discrimination is a bit challenging for Blaze, but Brie has no worries. She knows that with their strong relationship, they will work through any difficulties.

Brie and Blaze compete in AKC, UKC, and CKC obedience; AKC rally; and CPE agility. She hopes to start competing in AKC agility soon. She also does 4-H and is training Blaze and Buzz for freestyle and flyball. She shows Buzz in Junior Showmanship.

"Blaze and I are an awesome team; we are very tuned in to each other. I feel as though he understands what I expect of him all the time and tries his best in doing it. He is very willing to please me," says Brie. It sure sounds like Brie has her dream dog!

8

Finding Your Roots

In history class, you learn about the history of human beings and many different events that occurred in the past. You should also try to learn about your dog's breed. Among other things, find out what your dog was originally bred to do. For example, Pembroke Welsh Corgis were bred to herd cattle, and Rhodesian Ridgebacks were bred to hunt lions. After you find out what your dog was bred to do, you will probably find that there is a modern sport very similar to that original purpose. So start your research.

The Draft Dog Sports

Some of the most fun activities involve dogs who are capable and willing to pull us or other things along. Think back to the pictures of dogs pulling travois for the Native Americans in your history books. All you need is a dog, a harness made for pulling, and something to pull—even if it is just you on a pair of skis!

Don't underestimate your small dog, either—Kate's Corgi, Flash, is an accomplished carting dog—even if all she pulls is a small chariot! Still, the best dogs for pulling sports are the Northern breeds developed for pulling sleds and some of the strong Working and Terrier breeds such as American Staffordshire Terriers and Newfoundlands. The sledding breeds have generations of inborn pulling urges and the desire to run. This can make them challenging obedience dogs, but they excel out here doing what they were designed to do.

Your mixed breed may turn out to be a stellar pulling dog, too, especially if she has a mix of some of the strong breeds with a desire to pull or run. The

Alaskan Husky, which is the type of dog most Iditarod competitors use, is a custom mix of a wide variety of breeds and types to create an incredibly sound, tough, fast running dog. Lab mixes often make good pulling dogs, too, as well as any mix with a wide, strong chest.

After you have a good harness, you need to teach your dog to pull weight and to move out ahead of you. For carting, you can have your dog on a leash, but for sports like skijoring (where the dog is pulling you on skis) and sledding, your dog needs to be willing to run out ahead of you and keep going. It works best if you have a helper to ski or run out ahead and call your dog at first. Gradually, she will learn to run when told to do so. You can teach a Stop command and right and left turns while on leash so you have some control. If you know someone with a trained sledding or skijoring dog, you may find that partnering the dogs up will help teach your dog the ropes.

It is important that any dog who is asked to pull be physically fit and sound. No extra weight is important, and good conformation with normal hips, elbows, and stifles really make this sport fun for your dog. Start gradually with an exercise program.

For pulling any weight, whether it is a loaded "boat" for a weight pull or you on cross-country skis, your dog needs to gradually build up muscle and stamina. Asking too much too soon could lead to injuries and make your dog decide that these sports just aren't fun.

Make sure that you purchase safe, sensible equipment (see our resources in Apendixes A and C), but realize that here is your chance to check out wild colors for your harness, and you can decorate your cart or sled. Our carts have been decorated as Santa's transport and patriotic themes, and once as

Sled races are a fun family winter sport.

Organizations

There are a number of different groups that offer draft dog competitions. These groups may offer training classes, clinics, and seminars as well.

- **United Kennel Club** (weight pulls)
- **International Weight Pull Association**
- **ISDRA** (International Sled Dog Racing Association)
- **IFSS** (International Federation of Sleddog Sports)
- **North American Skijoring and Ski Pulk Association**

a fire engine! Carts and sleds can be purchased or homemade from plans. We have two carts—one we purchased and one we made ourselves.

Carting, sledding, and skijoring can be just for fun at home, or you can head out to competitions. The photo on page 94 shows how much fun these dogs are having! While some breed clubs hold events just for their breed, UKC and many private clubs welcome all breeds and mixed breeds at their events. We have seen skijoring competitions with dogs ranging from Flat-Coated Retrievers to Akitas and Border Collies with many dogs in between. There is even a sled team of Poodles!

Rottweilers, Bernese Mountain Dogs, Saint Bernards, Great Pyrenees, Newfoundlands, and Collies all have breed-specific carting titles. The Canadian Kennel Club offers all breed titles, and more carting clubs are forming. Some Northern breed clubs offer sledding, weight pull, and draft titles. Weight pull and carting trials usually adjust the required weight your dog must move by a percentage of body weight. So don't worry that your Chihuahua mix might have to pull 500 lbs.

Herding

Many breeds, such as Pembroke Welsh Corgis and Border Collies, were bred to herd stock animals. Some originally brought cattle to market; others kept a shepherd's flock from wandering off. Today, there are competitive herding events offered by the American Kennel Club (AKC), the Australian Shepherd Club of America (ASCA), the American Herding Breeds Association (AHBA), and others. These competitions are usually held in arenas, although some take place in open fields.

Many breeds can compete in herding trials. These include the AKC's entire Herding Group as well as some other breeds that have been approved for herding over the years, such as Samoyeds and Rottweilers. Soft Coated Wheaten Terriers and Giant and Standard Schnauzers are a few of the more recent additions. The Canadian Kennel Club accepts other breeds that were

"born to herd," such as the Kelpie, which is not recognized by the AKC. They even allow nontraditional breeds, such as Poodles and Doberman Pinschers, to compete.

Depending on your interests, you may want to compete in herding or just do it for fun. If you live on or near a farm, your well-trained Australian Cattle Dog may be greatly appreciated. Many dogs help out with work around the farm, guiding stock to and from pasture, rounding up any strays, and in general making life easier. The photo on page 97 shows Hokey calmly working our sheep at home. If you do decide you want to compete, look into multiple organizations. AKC, AHBA, and ASCA are the three main organizations that offer herding trials and titles for qualifying runs. Many Border Collie organizations also hold trials, some of which are limited to their breed. There are many levels of competition, and you should look into the requirements that your dog will have to meet to qualify before you enter a trial.

Many different types of stock can be used for herding, but there are three main favorites. Sheep are the most popular type of stock, and almost all trials offer classes with sheep. For those who prefer a slightly less imposing animal, ducks are gaining in popularity, although they can be quite difficult to work and require great patience on the part of both you and your dog. And for the true herdsmen and women out there, some trials also offer cattle. As you know, cattle are fairly large and therefore are less concerned about a human in their path than sheep or ducks, particularly when there is a dog racing behind them.

Each organization has multiple levels of competition, but virtually all start with a simple instinct test or relatively easy pass/fail herding test. The exception is ASCA, where competition starts right out at the trial level. ASCA does offer special junior classes, so this can be a great way for kids to start, with a separate class just on the junior's handling ability.

Communicating with Your Herding Dog

Herding dogs work off a number of signals. They respond to your verbal commands, to whistles, to the movement of your crook, and to the movements of the livestock. Working on instinct, some herding dogs fetch livestock to you; others drive it away from you; and some will act as a "living fence"—keeping livestock confined while they graze.

Herding as it should be—a calm walk for shepherd, sheep, and dog.

Most families are not going to go out and buy sheep or ducks for their dog, although our family did! You need to inquire about herding classes in your area and then make sure the instructor is willing to take on a novice, especially if you are a kid and your dog is not a Border Collie. Many instructors limit themselves as to what breeds of dog they are comfortable working with. It is best if your dog has had some obedience training before you head into herding, as an uncontrolled dog can cause damage to the livestock, you, and herself. Sort of like in medicine, the first rule of herding is to do no harm.

Earthdog Activities: A Job for a Digger!

If your dog is a small terrier or a Dachshund, earthdog trials may be the ideal dog sport for you! These breeds were developed to hunt small prey such as vermin, chase them to "ground" or into their dens, and then dig them out. Before you start feeling squeamish, especially if you have a pet rat, be assured that no rats are hurt in these trials.

For earthdog trials, special dens are made—tunnels that are carefully dug and packed so they won't cave in on your dog and with exit arrangements so the cage of rats and your dog can be safely and easily removed. The rats are kept in a safe cage, so while they may get barked at, they won't get hurt. And what is a little noise if you get great food and good care the rest of the time?

Going into a hole in the ground knowing you are heading for a tough customer like a rat requires instinct and courage. These small terriers and Dachshunds are calling on many generations of genetic programming to work this way. The dog must find and enter the tunnel, make her way past

Earthdog Titles

AKC's earthdog titles go from JE for Junior Earthdog to ME for Master Earthdog, in which a dog must track the prey, indicate and enter the tunnel, and work companionably with a fellow dog. Some breed clubs offer their own hunting programs as well.

false turns, and head for the rat cage within a specific amount of time. She then has to bark to alert that she has made a find and stay steady until told to leave.

The UKC offers an Earthwork Program and also programs for Feists—working terriers and curs. There are families who do actually hunt with their small terriers and Dachshunds in the tradition of the breeds. These hardy little dogs are excellent for pest control on farms, and Dachshunds are also used as "blood trailers"—following the blood drops and scent from wounded prey such as deer so that hunters can humanely kill them and not leave them to lingering deaths. Big, tough jobs for small dogs!

A-Hunting We Will Go

Just as there are many different breeds and types of hunting dogs, there are a wide variety of hunt tests and field trials for sporting dogs and hounds. Don't expect your Basset Hound to leap into the water to retrieve a duck, or your Labrador Retriever to steadily point a pheasant. Breeds hunt different species and in different ways. Although organized hunts can't exactly equal real hunting conditions, they do try to test whether or not your dog retains the instincts her breed was developed for.

Many families hunt with their dogs on their own as well as participate in organized competitions. Grouse, duck, goose, and pheasant can all be welcome additions to the menu in these homes.

Demonstrating obedience to command is very important in many of these competitions. Also, while many herding dogs work alone, hunting dogs often work as pairs or in packs. They must get along with the dogs they work with.

You, yourself, do not need to know how to shoot, as there are official guns. Some working tests and hunt tests use birds that are already dead, and test organizers are very conscientious about not leaving wounded birds or animals. If you aren't comfortable with working with live (or previously live) prey, you can train and work your dog with boat bumpers or dummies.

Organizations offering hunting tests include the AKC, the UKC, and many individual breed clubs. Tests are always designed for a group or specific breed. Retrievers must have water and land parts to their tests, but pointers can stay on dry land. The basic groups of hunting dogs are scenthounds, pointers, retrievers, spaniels, and sighthounds. Sighthounds are discussed under lure coursing.

Scenthounds

Scenthounds include familiar breeds like Beagles and Basset Hounds. These two breeds have organized field trials working rabbits. They have to demonstrate that they will *give voice*, which is barking to let the hunter know they are on the scent of game; they must trail the game; and they must be willing to run and show their endurance and persistence. Many families run their Beagles just for the fun of watching them work.

> **Hunting Goals**
>
> All hunting dogs are judged on *mouth*—meaning how nicely they carry the dead bird. A bird that is chewed up or torn will not be suitable for eating. Wounded birds must also be found and retrieved so they can be humanely killed. The goal here is to have a dog and human partnership that brings home supper.

Coonhounds

Coonhounds are another group of scenting hounds with organized competitions. The UKC even offers youth competitions. In real coon hunting, a wild raccoon is found and treed. In organized competitions, very often a trail is laid with raccoon scent and the actual raccoon is safely ensconced in a cage either in a tree or over water. The hounds must *give tongue*, that distinctive hound call that says they are working, follow the scent, and find the quarry.

The Pointing Group

The pointing group of dogs include setters, the pointing breeds like German Shorthairs and Vizslas, and Weimaraners. The AKC offers both hunt tests for the average hunter and his dogs and field trials for the serious competitor. Pointing breeds must show a point, of course! These dogs should also be steady to *wing*—when the bird they find flies up—and to *shot*—remaining steady while the hunter shoots the game. So they find birds, point them out to their human partner, wait until the bird is shot, and then go retrieve it. Pointing breeds are often worked in pairs or braces and must *honor* each other—backing the other dog up if she finds a bird first.

> **Having a Soft Mouth**
>
> All of the bird-hunting dogs should have a soft mouth so their birds are not chewed and not be gunshy or panic when a gun is shot off near them. Many trainers start small puppies off by letting them hear gunshots and encouraging them to retrieve carefully.

An enthusiastic Lab, doing what he was bred for!

Retrievers

Retrievers are the classic duck-hunting dog, but they can work on land or in water. For many competitions, these dogs must demonstrate their ability to do both—even if it is cold and the water is icy. Although Goldens and Labs are the best known retriever breeds, Flat Coats, Chesapeake Bays, and Curly Coats are among the other good retrieving breeds recognized. Retrievers also have to be able to *mark* birds—that is, remember where the shot duck went down so they can find it when they are sent. Advanced tests also require dogs to do *blind* retrieves when the dog has not seen where the duck fell, but is guided by you. Dogs also have to do doubles, where they are sent for one bird and then must go get a second as well. The photo shows a Labrador Retriever happily working for his handler.

Many retriever breed clubs have their own working certificates, which are easier than hunt tests or field trials so that families can demonstrate that their dog does retain her retrieving instincts. Some clubs allow dogs to show off their abilities using boat bumpers or dummies instead of real birds. Both the AKC and the UKC have big hunting retriever programs. NAHRA is the North American Hunting Retriever Association. This group takes the preservation of hunting instincts in their dogs very seriously and runs competitions as well.

Spaniels

Spaniels are known for their bouncy gait and jumping abilities, which fit in with their style of hunting. Spaniel breeds include the English Springer Spaniel and the American Cocker Spaniel, as well as several other breeds. Spaniels were bred to *flush* birds—by locating them first by scent and then pouncing to make them fly up. The hunter could then shoot them, and the spaniels would retrieve them for supper. Spaniels are also expected to work both on land and in water and to have a *soft mouth* so the birds are not chewed up.

In spaniel hunt tests or field trials, the dogs must find the birds by scenting and then flush them up for the hunter. After the birds are shot, the dogs must locate them and retrieve them to the hunter. Some tests may use birds that are already dead, but they can still be used to demonstrate water retrieves. Breed clubs may hold their own working tests, and the AKC has a hunt test program for spaniel breeds.

Road Trials: Dogs on the Move

If you look at old photos, you may see a Dalmatian trotting calmly alongside a carriage or running next to a horseback rider. This was before Dalmatians became fire truck mascots, of course, but they did ride along on the horse-drawn fire wagons.

The Dalmatian Club of America decided to prove that their breed can still do its original function: travel along with their owners, staying with the carriage and horses to keep them safe while traveling, and guarding the carriage and horses in the stables along the way. So they came up with Road Trials.

There are two levels of Road Trials: Road Dog with a 12½-mile course and Road Dog Excellent with a 25-mile course. For both of these courses, the dog must accompany either a rider on horseback or a horse-drawn carriage. (Obviously, you must like horses to try this sport.) The dog must stay in position near the horse or carriage, not interfering and not being distracted. A couple of obedience exercises are also included. There are veterinary checks along the way to make sure your horse and dog are not lame or under any physical stress.

While only Dalmatians can earn titles for this work, almost any dog can be trained to go with you when you ride your horse. You need to have a horse who is comfortable around dogs and a dog who will not try to nip or herd the horse. Even herding dogs can be trained to make good trail-riding buddies; our Belgian Tervurens, our Aussies, and even the Corgis go with us on rides. Your dog will probably need some solid obedience training, too. Leaving your side to chase deer, other animals, or cars is not acceptable.

For Parents Only

After your kids get into the wonderful world of dogs, there is no end to the sports they can try. Many organizations offer junior divisions or special awards for junior competitors. These are family-oriented activities, and they put heavy emphasis on safety. The activities listed here can be useful in real life as well.

Our dogs work our sheep and ducks. They pull carts and sleds with hay or bedding and participate in parades and fundraisers with their carts. They hunt mice in the barn and fields. Although we don't have any bird dogs, we know people who depend on their dogs to help put meat on the supper table.

These activities can also all be done just for fun and the joy of seeing the true talents of your dog come shining forth. Whether done in actual competition or just training on your own, you develop a special bond with your dog when you work together doing what she was selected to do for many generations. The instincts are often there, just waiting under the surface for the chance to be demonstrated.

Training in these sports can be expensive, both for the cost of classes and the equipment. Although hunt tests training may require only some boat bumpers or bird wings, many herding enthusiasts eventually end up with livestock of their own. Entry fees are often higher for these tests, due to the increased costs of arranging them, compared to obedience or agility fees. Local clubs may give price breaks to juniors for training and in competitions. And remind your kids that exhibitors are often expected to help out in some way. Kids who are helpers are always welcome and may earn discounts.

Lure Coursing: The Canine Cheetahs

Lure coursing is a sport developed to show off the instincts and talents of sighthounds. These breeds hunt by spotting game and running it down. They are very alert to movements and very fast—sprinters much like cheetahs. Breeds here include Greyhounds, Salukis, Irish Wolfhounds, Basenjis, and some other hound breeds.

Obviously, there is a wide range of sizes in this group, with very different original prey species. Since finding gazelle or wolves to hunt would be difficult, the clubs have come up with a simple solution to test the running and visual tracking abilities of their dogs. A lure course is set up using pulleys with a bright white bag or cloth as the prey. The dogs must run the course, not cheating and cutting corners and not bothering the other dogs running with them. The course is set up with turns and twists to simulate an escaping prey animal.

In lure coursing, the dog must show its speed, ability to turn, persistence in continuing to follow the lure, and endurance. At the upper levels, the dog must be able to run with other dogs peaceably.

Racing Greyhounds and Whippets also chase a lure—this time around a circular track with a group of other dogs. Many ex-racers make wonderful pets and can go lure coursing in their new homes.

The two main organizations for lure coursing are the AKC and ASFA—American Sighthound Field Association. These groups offer titles but also field championships for the dogs who truly exemplify the working abilities of a sighthound. An FC denotes a field championship.

Although not that many people still actively hunt with their sighthounds, there are people who open field hunt. These sighthounds may be turned loose to run jackrabbits or other prey. NOFCA is the National Open Field Coursing Association, and they hold trials, mainly in the western part of the United States, to test their sighthounds under true hunting conditions.

Profile: Sarah and Sooner

Sarah had wanted a dog of her own for many years—her mom has had dogs and trained and shown them. Although those dogs had always been part of Sarah's family, she wanted a dog of her very own.

One day her mom picked her up from a friend's house and out of the blue said, "A friend of mine knows someone selling a year-old Cardigan Corgi. Do you want to check it out?" The very next day they drove to Pennsylvania to get Sooner. Sarah was 15 years old, and Sooner was exactly 1 year old. Buying Sooner was Sarah's best purchase ever.

Since Sarah was older when she got Sooner, all of Sooner's care was her responsibility right from the start. "I am completely responsible for my dog, like feeding, bathing, exercising, and whatever else she needs, so really I don't get help caring for her." Being completely responsible for Sooner's care helped Sarah form a quick and very tight bond with Sooner.

It has been easy for Sarah to train Sooner. Being a little older, Sooner had more of an attention span than a young puppy. Their tight bond has made them a real team. Some of the easiest things for Sarah to teach Sooner have been to spin and to spin into heel position. Herding sheep is harder—like many Corgis, Sooner is tough when it comes to livestock!

Sooner is a very special dog to Sarah for many reasons. As she goes through those tough teenage years, she has one ultimate ally. "Sooner is special because she is my best friend. No matter how much I push her away at times, she is always right there, with lots of kisses. I also use her as a judge of character when meeting new people. She knows if someone is good or bad the minute she meets them, and if they are bad, she will let me know. Sooner is smart that way!"

Sooner is Sarah's canine guardian.

One of the best things about Sooner for Sarah is her protectiveness. "Sooner is like my guardian. I feel safe in the dark when she is around because she lets everyone and everything know that I am hers and that they will have to get through her before they get to me!" A dog is a constant guardian, and in our world, which can be frightening at times, your beloved dog is always there and on alert.

Sarah and Sooner do many things together. They hike, jog, camp, swim, herd, and attend festivals (remember that well-trained dog advice!), and are great in agility. One of their favorite activities is just hanging out at home and wrestling together.

The only drawback to having a dog of her own is that Sarah is now facing going off to college and will probably have to leave Sooner at home. That will be hard for both of them, even though Sarah will know her dog is in capable hands.

Sarah feels that Sooner has added immeasurably to her life. "My dog is a super awesome dog, and I can honestly say I'd be lost without her. She has given me two great years so far, and I know the rest of her life we'll spend together. I thank her for being mine!"

9

Extracurricular Activities: Sports

Just like many kids enjoy sports or gym class, dogs enjoy similar activities, too. And even if you aren't a sports star, you can still have fun with your dog. These activities are a great way to keep your dog fit and in shape. It's good for you, too. Although many of these dog sports have organized competitions, you and your dog can just enjoy doing them at class or at home if that is all you want. It may take a superstar to shine in some of these activities, but any dog can play at some level.

Agility

If you ever watch Animal Planet, you've probably seen the competitions where dogs run through tunnels, jump over bars, and leap through tires. This sport is called *agility*. Basically, agility is an obstacle course for your dog to complete. Most dogs love this, and it is a great way to keep your dog fit.

Some of the obstacles found on an agility course are tunnels (open and closed), jumps, tires, teeter-totters, dogwalks, A-frames, weave poles, and tables. Tunnels are a big hit in the canine world, and even a little puppy can learn to do them. Open tunnels are basically giant tubes that the dog gets to run through, and closed tunnels are barrels with a cloth chute at the end. The closed tunnel is a little trickier because your dog can't see where he is going.

This Greyhound does the dogwalk despite the distraction of the cows nearby.

For working on your own, you don't need a full set of equipment. Some weave poles, even just stick–in-the-ground stakes, and a couple of jumps will be an excellent start. Many people save up for a tunnel, and true agility addicts will eventually make or buy contact obstacles such as the teeter-totter and dogwalk.

Jumps are fairly self-explanatory and can have up to three bars. A tire is a raised hoop for your dog to jump through. The teeter-totter, dogwalk, and A-frame are all known as contacts because of the yellow zone at each end that your dog must put at least one paw into. A teeter-totter will tip when your dog reaches the halfway point; a dogwalk looks like a bridge; and an A-frame looks like a giant letter A. As you can see in the photo, this Greyhound can handle the dogwalk just fine even though she is a big dog. Weave poles are one of the more difficult obstacles to teach your dog, for he has to weave between up to twelve poles without stopping or skipping a pole. For the table, all your dog has to do is jump up on it and do a Sit or Down Stay for five seconds. Some competitive organizations have other obstacles, but these are the basics.

Contact Zones

Although it may seem at times that contact zones are simply there to challenge you and your dog, they are actually designed for safety. If your dog puts a paw or two in the contact zone, she isn't leaping off crazily and possibly injuring herself. Some dogs do seem to feel the color change marks the place to leap from, though!

If you want to do agility just for fun, you can do almost anything. You can invent new obstacles for your dog to try out, and maybe even get together with other kids in your neighborhood to see whether their dogs like agility.

But almost everyone who tries out agility ends up competing at some time or another. If you decide that you want to compete, your best bet is to sign up for a class. Follow the same guidelines as when you look for an obedience instructor. Safety and fun are very important. Make sure the class has some control so you don't have highly excited dogs running loose every which way. After you and your dog have gone through classes and can run a series of obstacles, you can start looking into the organizations that offer competitions.

The American Kennel Club (AKC) is one of the most prominent organizations that offers agility. The North American Dog Agility Council (NADAC), Canine Performance Events (CPE), and the United States Dog Agility Association (USDAA) are three other popular groups that focus on agility. CPE is one of the best for a beginner because it is very laid back, and the lower levels are fairly simple. NADAC and USDAA are also good for beginners, and all three have good junior programs. The AKC offers a Junior Recognition program that can make you eligible for scholarships later. The UKC also has an agility program that focuses on control a bit more than some of the other groups and less on speed, so if you have a slow-but-steady agility dog, it may be the venue for you.

This young Dalmatian is starting out on "baby" agility equipment.

You can compete in many different classes as well. The lowest level is traditionally Novice, with upper levels varying depending on the organization. Most venues offer a Standard or Regular class that includes all of the obstacles and even the contacts. Jumpers, which has everything except the contacts and table, is another class included in almost every venue. NADAC has classes that focus on different obstacles, including Tunnelers, which is our dogs' favorite class. This class is perfect for young dogs and older dogs because the course is made up entirely of tunnels. Some of the venues also offer strategic games that require a little more thinking on the part of the handler.

Whether you do agility for fun or to compete, you need to keep it safe for your dog. When you first start teaching her to jump, start low and gradually raise the bar. The photo on page 107 shows a neat set of baby agility equipment for young dogs. Dogs under a year of age shouldn't jump anything above the height of their elbow, and be aware that an older dog may have trouble with high jumps or the A-frame.

Flying through the Air: Disc Chasing

If snowboarders are extreme human athletes, then dogs who chase and catch discs are extreme canine athletes. Still, although it takes an incredible athlete to shine in this sport, any dog who likes to retrieve can enjoy it. Dog disc sports started out with the well-known Frisbee, but now there are a wide range of discs for dogs to fetch, including some custom made for dog sports (see our resources in Appendixes A, B, and C).

At the most basic level, you throw the disc, and your dog runs to fetch it and brings it back, handing it to you. Of course, this means that *you* have to be decent at throwing the disc. We admit to being throwing challenged and have had to climb on the roof more than once to retrieve our discs ourselves! For simply running on the flat, your dog needs to be reasonably fit and ideally not overweight. However, dogs with long backs are better off staying on the ground.

For a puppy whom you don't want injuring joints, just rolling a disc on the ground is a great way to start. Older dogs enjoy this, too, and may pounce on the disc when they catch it.

If your dog is not reliable about bringing the disc back to you, you may want to start out by putting a long line on her. This should be something light, like parachute cord, but be sure to wear gloves, as this can cord give you rope burns. Do the trade trick as well. When your dog brings you the disc, trade her something great like a really good treat. She will quickly learn that the faster she brings the disc back to you, the faster she gets the goody.

Many dogs quickly learn this game and decide to beat the disc to the ground by catching it in the air. If you think Michael Jordan can catch air, you should see

Deciding on a Disc

A huge number of discs are available for your dog to retrieve. The hard plastic ones that can get brittle with age and sun or exposure to cold are out. Most dogs prefer a soft plastic, rubber, or cloth disc as it is easier on their teeth.

these dogs! Clever dogs learn to follow the pattern of the disc and intercept it—sometimes right before it lands so they barely get all four feet off the ground, or sometimes way up in the air, with spectacular leaps and spins.

In disc dog competitions, there are usually multiple types of events. Some simply time how many retrieves your dog can make in a specified period. The throws must go a minimum distance as well. Others require your dog to retrieve throws that land in a specific zone—this is where your throwing expertise becomes important. Depending on the organization, your dog may be required to have all four paws off the ground at the time of the catch. Whether his paws are 4 inches or 4 feet off the ground doesn't matter, just that he is truly airborne!

Some of the most exciting disc dog competitions are freestyle events. With background music chosen by the competitor, the dog and handler team do an original timed routine using throws of the disc, tricks, and teamwork. Some routines even have the dog launch off the handler for spectacular flying catches!

At all times, disc dog competitions emphasize the safety of your dog and stress that you need to be aware of what condition your dog is in and whether she is physically capable of doing this sport. Most competitions specify that only certain discs be used, and great research has gone into these discs to determine the best ones for aerodynamic flight plus ease of catching for your dog—without damaging her mouth or teeth.

Remember, one of the key elements in this sport is that your dog runs right out, gets the disc, and returns it to you—ideally handing it to you. Some dogs like to tease you by staying just out of reach with the disc. Others run off altogether, with the disc as their prize. And a few dogs bring you the disc but won't let go, so you end up in a tug of war. None of those versions will be very good if you want to compete. Still, for backyard fun, all is fair.

For the dogs who love to leap, spin, and even somersault while in the air, like Tom's dog Baloo, *you* have to be conscious of safety at all times. (See chapter 1 for more on Tom and Baloo.) Make sure the footing is good for your dog. Don't overdo those impressive leaps. Keep your dog fit by having her run or swim, and make sure her figure is trim. In hot weather, take precautions to avoid heatstroke—plenty of rest in the shade and lots of fresh, cool water.

Flyball—a Team Sport for Ball-Crazy Dogs

Your average ball-crazy kid has plenty of sports options: soccer, baseball, basketball, and so on. For the ball-crazy dog, flyball is a really fun team sport. Again, you may have seen this on Animal Planet or ESPN.

The game of flyball is simple. You have four dogs on a team who run one at a time. Each team has its own lane with four jumps and a special box at the end. Your dog must run down the lane and over all four jumps and hit a release on the box so that a tennis ball comes out. She snags the ball, turns, and comes back over the four jumps. As soon as she crosses the finish line, the next teammate goes. *Very* fast, very fun, and usually very noisy!

The field is set up with 6 feet from the start line to the first jump, 10 feet between the next three jumps, and finally 15 feet to the box. Since at least two teams run at once, side by side, your dog *must not* be aggressive to other dogs and must concentrate and stay in his lane. Stealing balls from the other team is frowned upon as well, even if your dog beats the other dog down to the boxes. Most dogs bark and shriek while watching or running, so you may want earplugs if you go to watch.

> **How High to Fly**
>
> Jump heights for a team are based on the height of the shortest dog on the team. Jump heights range from 8 to 16 inches. Fast, small dogs are very desirable on teams, as that means the whole team can do the shortest jump possible. Jack/Parson Russell Terriers are top flyball dogs!

The boxes are set to release balls at a certain angle each time. This is great for dogs who can't catch very well, as they learn exactly where the ball will appear and simply open their mouths wide!

Flyball sites often have plans for building equipment so you can do this sport fairly inexpensively (see Appendixes A, B, and C). And, of course, with a team, you can share entry fees, equipment, and driving.

Although being on a flyball team is extra fun, this is a sport you also can do at home just for fun. After you have a box, you can make jumps out of almost anything, or even skip the jumps if your dog doesn't like to jump.

Flyball is a wonderful sport to do for demonstrations. You can involve spectators as ball loaders for the box, and everyone loves to cheer and remark on how clever your dog is to work the ball release.

Water Sports

There are a number of breeds and mixed breeds who simply love being in the water, swimming and retrieving or even diving. Some breed clubs have special water tests for their breeds, like the Newfoundlands and Portuguese Water Dogs, but any dog can train and do these things for fun or go for national fame on the Great Outdoor Games!

All the water work tests for most groups emphasize the importance of basic control. If your dog won't listen to you and respond to your commands, he is not ready to work off leash and in the water. Hopefully, you did your homework and can now try some fun water sports.

You may have seen sports shows with crazy people diving off huge cliffs into the ocean. Well, DockDogs, also called Big Air, leap off a dock, launching themselves after a thrown object with similar panache. If you have a dog who loves leaping into lakes, ponds, or your pool, this is the sport for you.

The goal is that the dog must run to the end of the dock and leap into the water after a thrown object—often a ball or boat bumper. A retrieve is not required, and placements and titles are based on the length of the jump from the edge of the dock to where the dog's body breaks the water. Regulation docks are 40 feet long and 8 feet wide, raised 24 inches off the water. Good footing is a must!

As the handler, you must be able to control your dog, have him run in a straight line at speed off the dock, and be able to throw well. Yes, it's another dog sport where *you* may have to practice your throwing on your own!

DockDog titles start from Novice Jumper and go to Elite Jumper, with five qualifying legs required based on the distance jumped. This sport has caught on fire, and after just a few years it already has national championships and big sponsorships. All dogs are welcome, and juniors may compete as well.

Dock Dogs

Although many of the top DockDogs are Labrador Retrievers, you will see other retriever breeds, mixed breeds, and dogs of other breeds out competing. All you really need is a dog who loves running, jumping, and water!

The Newfoundland Club of America has special water work tests designed to test the basic water rescue talents of Newfs, but any dog can train and practice these techniques. Kate's Corgi Flash can do all the basic exercises and will actually tow a person to shore! So don't dismiss this fun just because you don't own a Newf.

Swimming Together

Learning to swim with a handler is important for any dog who might swim with you. A dog who swims out to you and tries to climb on you will leave you with horrible scratches and might even force you under the water. You want your dog nearby but swimming on his own.

The basic ideas with the Newf club program are that the dog should be able to retrieve from the water and bring the object to your hand, take lifesaving devices out to swimmers, tow a boat, and swim safely with her handler. Warning—once your dog has mastered these tasks, she may keep trying to rescue you from your leisurely swim in the lake or splash into your pool!

In the Newf tests, your dog is required to retrieve and/or deliver lifesaving devices like a ring, life jacket, or boat cushion. By delivering the life-saving equipment, your dog gives a person having trouble in the water a way to stay afloat. He can then tow you back to shore—with you holding his tail or a line or him holding you by your arm. He will even have to go underwater to retrieve objects thrown in shallow water. Your dog must also be comfortable and well behaved while riding in a boat. A trained water rescue dog is a lifeguard who won't be distracted by cute girls in bikinis or ask for a raise each summer.

Portuguese Water Dogs have different water tasks. They have to retrieve fishing nets, lay out buoys, retrieve objects from the water as well as underwater, and carry courier pouches for communication between boats. As with the Newf rules, the dog must also swim with the handler in a safe manner.

These dogs also have to be willing to ride in a boat in a quiet and well-behaved manner and to obey commands from other people. This way, if you sent your dog with a pouch to a distant boat, he will deliver it, and then might be given another object and be commanded by a stranger to bring it to you.

Water Dogs Extraordinaire

The Portuguese Water Dog titles include Courier Water Dog and Junior Water Dog designations, as well as advanced titles in these areas and Versatility awards. Although other breeds won't get the titles, they can still train in all the exercises.

Clearly, these tasks can be fun for any dog and useful for a family. You could send your dog to deliver a message saying it is time to row in for lunch or have him place markers for a game of water polo.

With the popularity of water sports for so many dogs, an organization was started to encourage water

Finding Water Training Info

Water organizations have rules and regulations as well as training manuals and articles that can be ordered or printed off the Internet so that you can work on your own. Just because you don't own a Newf doesn't mean you can't use the manual to train your large water hound! Many clubs also offer seminars and will allow other dogs if there is space.

work and training for all dogs, including mixed breeds. WETDOG, or Water Education and Training Dog Obedience Group, has taken parts of the various water work tests and made their own titling levels so that any dog can earn his "water wings" and prove he is a safe companion around the water.

Tracking: Born to Sniff

Does your dog spend 90 percent of her time with her nose on the ground? Then tracking is the sport for you! Tracking is perfect for dogs of all ages since it requires the one thing that all dogs love to do—sniff. Dogs also enjoy tracking because they are in charge. After all, we don't think *you* are going to run around smelling the ground to track a scent! If you have ever thought about doing search and rescue work, tracking is a great first step.

Tracking can be done on your own or through a class. There are many excellent books on tracking for all levels of expertise.

The basic pieces of equipment that you will need are a harness that is not restrictive so your dog can move easily, a 40-foot line (nylon or parachute

This Golden Retriever shows strong tracking instinct.

Tracking Opportunities

The AKC tracking program is just for purebred dogs, but the ASCA program is open to all breeds and to mixed breeds, with preference for the limited test spots to Australian Shepherds. Kate's Corgi has both an ASCA and AKC TD. TD is for Tracking Dog, the first level.

cord works well), an article for your dog to find, such as a glove or a slipper, and some flags to mark the start and turns until you get more experienced. The ideal situation would team you up with an experienced partner who can teach you about laying tracks, while at the same time teaching your dog how to run them. The photo on page 113 shows a dog who is trained and starting on a track at a test.

The goal in tracking is for your dog to follow someone's path and find anything of theirs they leave along the way. Your dog must stick to the path of that one person you designate. Initially tracks are only a few minutes old, but eventually, your dog will follow tracks that are hours old. It is best to start on grass, but top dogs can also track across pavement and asphalt.

Along with being a neat way to compete with your dog, tracking can be useful. Our dogs have found keys, mittens, and hats left behind by people. Tracking is also a good sport for both young and old dogs as it is not stressful on the joints. Your dog is always on the long line, so if he is not the best about coming when called, he can still compete in tracking.

Hiking and Backpacking: Taking to the Great Outdoors

One of the best ways to enjoy your dog's company is to go on a hike together. With a well-fitted backpack, your dog can even carry her own water, snacks, and first-aid kit. And a big dog might carry enough for you to share! The photo on page 115 shows a dog with a well-fitting day pack for short hikes.

There are organizations that offer hiking titles, and many Web sites sell patches for your mileage accomplishments, but most hikers simply do this on their own with no thought of recognition. Backpacks can be homemade or purchased at many different sites. The best backpack manufacturers request some measurements to be sure the pack will fit your dog comfortably.

Plan your trip carefully, taking into account the footing, such as climbing up the side of a mountain, and the distance you will be going. Your dog should not drink from streams along the way unless you treat the water. Just as you need to build up endurance, so does your dog. Even her footpads need to get tougher for long hikes. Some dogs will need to wear booties to protect their feet.

Hiking can be a wonderful experience—you and your dog heading down a trail in cool but sunny weather, a light breeze, no bugs. That, of course, is the dream hike. A hike may also take place in cold rain, extreme heat, up and down hills, or through mosquito havens. Be prepared just like the Boy Scouts! With careful planning, you and your dog can be comfortable and have a great time.

One thing to research ahead of time is whether the park or area you plan to hike in allows dogs. *Always* respect park rules, or you could get dogs banned! Most parks will allow dogs on leash, and many beaches and forest areas do as well. Respect off-limits areas, such as beaches where there are nesting shore birds.

Kate and her Australian Shepherd are ready to hike with their homemade backpack.

Basic Trail Rules

There are a few basic, common-courtesy rules that all hikers follow. These rules are especially important if your dog is hiking with you.

- Have your dog on a 6-foot leash for her safety as well as courtesy.
- Clean up after your dog—bag or bury waste.
- Carry or treat water for her, just as you do for yourself.
- Gradually build up endurance for hikes.
- Use a top-quality backpack fitted to your dog.
- Gradually build up to full weight on a pack, which is 33 percent of their weight for most dogs.
- Have identification for your dog on her.
- Carry vaccination certificates.
- Have a good first-aid kit for both of you.
- Carry a map and/or a compass.

For Parents Only

The sports listed here range from expensive, equipment and training intensive, to simple and easy. There should be something here for every dog and handler team. You can be as competitive as you want with these sports or simply practice them at home for fun. Many books and Web sites have plans for building equipment, from flyball boxes to agility jumps. Use your imagination, too—a bench can be a dogwalk; toilet plungers make decent weave poles.

If you have only one family dog and two dog trainer kids, remember that sports like agility offer multiple runs per day. One child can be the jumper class specialist, and the other a standard class specialist. Dogs can and do adapt to multiple handlers. Our dogs have worked for both our kids as well as virtually all the kids in our 4-H club, plus an occasional kid at a dog event who didn't have a dog. A well-trained dog with a good temperament is a blessing.

A backyard disc dog star is just as significant to you as a national TV disc dog champion. Besides, too much glory may give your dog a swelled head, and he might start expecting even better room service than he already gets. If you want to shoot for the stars, though, these sports are open to everyone from beginners on up, and most competitors are very willing to help newcomers.

Hiking and water sport training are things that your whole family can enjoy. If you have a camp or vacation somewhere on the water, your dog will quickly learn to enjoy water sports—or at least riding on the boat.

Hiking is good exercise for everyone and can be lots of fun. I do advise you to avoid certain trails. We did a section of the Appalachian Trail near the Delaware Water Gap this summer in 90-degree heat, going straight up and down a hill—literally hanging onto trees. Although the dogs and kids thought it was a blast, *I* was less than thrilled.

Bottom line—find something you, your family, and your dog all enjoy and go for it!

There are many excellent hiking books and area guides for hikes that are dog friendly. Some local hiking clubs offer maps or guided tours to good hiking areas. Most hiking guides also rate trails as easy or difficult, discuss any special considerations, such as whether you need to climb a ladder, and give you distances. You may want to hike with a group or, if your dog gets too excited with other dogs, you may want to solo it. If you go solo, carry a cell phone and let someone know where you are going. Stay on the trails and follow markers!

Even if you and your dog are city slickers, you still have many hiking options. Most cities have some parks or nature trails that are open to dogs. Get a good pedometer, and your dog can rack up miles simply hiking city blocks. His 100-mile patch will be just as big an accomplishment as a dog who hikes 100 wilderness miles.

If you plan to take your dog camping, more preparations are in order. You need to pack carefully, considering his needs as well as yours, and be realistic about how much both of you can carry if you are backpacking to a site. Research your equipment carefully—collapsible water bowls are a recent and wonderful innovation for hikers. They are easy to pack, work well, and are light to carry.

Profile: Cecilia and Sage

Cecilia was 10 years old when she got her Pembroke Welsh Corgi, Sage. Her mother had previously worked at a kennel that raised Corgis, and the half-fluffy puppy soon became Cecilia's best friend. (Most Corgis have a fairly short but thick coat, while Sage has longer, fluffier hair.)

Right from the start, Cecilia took full responsibility for Sage's care and training, although she doesn't clip Sage's toenails. Many Corgis are less than thrilled about having their nails done, as Kate can attest with Flash. Since Sage is a half fluffy, she has longer, softer hair than most Corgis. Since she is also low to the ground, this means Cecilia really has to stay on top of her grooming.

Sage was very easy to train because she was willing to work and eager to please. Cecilia feels that Sit was the easiest thing to teach Sage. Cecilia is fairly tall and, of course, Sage is very short, so they had to develop teamwork so that Cecilia didn't have to always bend way over.

Over the years, Cecilia has taught Sage many new things, and they have competed successfully in many canine events. Sage is very smart and learns things quickly, which makes training fun for Cecilia . Sage is currently working on her Utility title—the hardest level of obedience training. Very few kids make it this far, especially with their first dog. Cecilia says, "Utility has been and still is very difficult," but we know they will persevere.

They also excel at agility, and Cecilia and Sage are one of the few junior handler teams to earn the Master Agility Champion title. This is a very difficult achievement, requiring your dog to have 20 double Qs, or qualifying runs, in both jumpers and standard at the most difficult level plus earn 750 points for speed. Not many dogs have the athletic ability to accomplish this feat, let alone with a kid for a handler. As you can see in the photo on page 118, Cecilia and Sage are a smooth team!

Cecilia and Sage wove their way to a MACH (Master Agility Champion) title.

Along with as obedience and agility, they compete in tracking and show in Grooming and Handling at the New York State Fair in 4-H. They have earned obedience and agility grand championships there, showing that small dogs can be mighty, too.

Cecilia says, "I think that Sage and I have a very solid relationship. I have made sure that I am 'top dog' from the start, so she knows I am the boss, but I think that's good. At the same time that she respects me, we can have a good time together." And that's just the way it should be!

10

Extracurricular Activities: Cultural Experiences

In your school, there are kids who excel in sports and those who don't. The same holds true for dogs: There are dogs who are superb athletes and dogs who aren't. That doesn't mean your dog isn't special, too, or that there aren't special activities for you and your dog to share. Although these activities may not have the excitement of a fast agility run, they still require effort and training. Doing a freestyle routine, gaiting your dog in juniors, or even showing off a cute trick are all events that may show off the special talents of your very special dog.

Breed Showing (aka Beauty Pageants)

Breed showing was originally intended as a way for breeders to look at the structure and temperament of dogs from their breed to pick the best dogs for breeding. Although that is still partly true, breed shows have taken on a life of their own. Proud owners often don't just show their dog to win a championship, but may continue to compete for national rankings. For the hard-core breed enthusiast, a professional handler may be hired to campaign their dog. We will assume that you are only interested in showing your dog yourself.

In breed competition, the judge has a picture in mind of the perfect dog of that breed. This picture is based on the *breed standard*—a blueprint for the breed that describes your dog's breed fully, from head to tail. The proper foot shape, the ideal tail, even which colors are acceptable are all included in the standard. Still, there is room for interpretation of the standard by the individual judge, which is why one dog may win today and a different dog tomorrow.

Small Dogs Need a Table

Small breeds of dogs are set up on a table for their examination. This saves the judge's back. You will need to practice picking your dog up safely and gracefully.

Most breed competitions require a dog to earn fifteen points to become a champion. The dog earns points by defeating other dogs. Most organizations also require that some of these points be earned in big chunks called majors. A *major* is when your dog defeats enough dogs to earn three or more points all at once. The number of dogs required for a major depends on the breed of dog and how popular it is. For less popular dogs, four or five total may be a major, but for popular breeds, it may take 20 or more dogs to have a major.

A show ring with lovely dogs on a sunny, breezy day is a beautiful sight.

Showing Different Breeds

Each breed is shown a bit differently. In some breeds, the tail is held up; in others, the tail is straight out; and in some, the tail is supposed to be down. Some breeds are *free baited,* in which the dog stands with no help from the handler—through a lot of training and practice—while other breeds are carefully *stacked,* with the handler placing each leg exactly where they want it. Watch your breed in the ring so you will know how your dog should be shown.

Owner-handlers are seen at dog shows, and they compete right against the professionals. It might be hard to tell the amateurs from the professionals in the photo on page 120. Although, theoretically, it is the dog being judged, not the handler, it is important that you become skilled enough to show off your dog's best points and not be a hindrance to her career. Many kennel clubs offer handling classes, and there are some excellent books on handling for conformation. A very good resource is your dog's breeder. She can guide you to helpful mentors in your area. Attending some dog shows as a spectator can be valuable, too—you can watch how the top handlers show your breed.

Dogs showing in breed must be purebred, so your mixed breed will have to settle for Junior Showmanship, which is fun, too (see the next section). Not all purebreds are show quality, either. A pet-quality dog could simply have white toes in a breed where they aren't allowed or possibly not have good structure. Be sure you know why your dog is classed as a pet if she is.

In most cases, your dog will have to be intact—not spayed or neutered—to show in conformation. ASCA is a wonderful exception, as they have a whole conformation program just for altered Australian Shepherds. This is a great chance for a nice dog to be shown but without the owners having to deal with the hassle of an intact male or a female in heat. Our two Aussies

The Dog Show Pyramid

Dog shows work as a pyramid. You start out competing against just the other dogs of your breed. Then the best dog of your breed competes against the other dogs in her group—for example, the Herding or Toy breeds. There are seven AKC Groups—Sporting, Hound, Working, Terrier, Non-Sporting, Toy, and Herding. The best dog from each group then goes on to try and win Best in Show.

show in the altered program. Some *specialty shows*—shows for just one breed—may offer special classes where spayed and neutered dogs can show in classes such as Veterans or Performance Titled.

The AKC and the UKC both offer extensive conformation events. You may have watched Westminster or the Eukanuba Championship on TV. Watch and listen closely; you will find many handlers are showing their own dogs, and there are often even some juniors showing dogs at these top events.

Modeling: Junior Showmanship

Junior Showmanship is one of the simplest things to teach your dog and yet is still a very competitive sport. Basically, it is the same as showing in breed—except now *you* are the one being judged.

Dogs love Juniors just because they hardly have to do anything and still get fed for it. Unlike obedience, where you are not allowed to carry food, it is very common in Juniors and breed. And if you're discreet, you can even have toys in the ring. All you need is a thin chain and leash or martingale for your dog and nice clothes for yourself. Most boys wear either a suit or dress slacks with a dress shirt. And yes, you do need a tie, although clip-ons are perfectly acceptable. For girls, a dress, slacks and a blouse, or a skirt and blouse are fine. If you decide to compete a lot, buying a nice skirt suit or pantsuit is a good idea. Whatever you decide to wear, pockets are a must. Some treats can be slipped under your armband, but pockets make life a lot easier.

Class procedure is generally the same. You will be called into the ring and asked to gait (note that your dog must be trotting) around the ring, and then each handler will be evaluated separately. For most dog breeds, to stack them, all you have to do is make sure that all four feet form a rectangle or

Appropriate Show Clothes

When planning your clothes for Junior Showmanship, think attractive but useful and comfortable. This is not a place for high-heeled shoes, low-cut blouses, or miniskirts. You will need to be able to bend over your dog without being embarrassed and to move as fast as your dog does—although that may be a fast walk for your Corgi, it could mean a run for your German Shepherd Dog. You also want to wear clothes in colors that complement your dog's—don't wear black pants with a black dog, as the dog will not stand out.

This young lady is just starting out in junior showmanship, while this boy is already an experienced showman.

square. Next, the judge will ask you for one of several patterns. The down and back, triangle, and L are the most common, although every now and then you might be asked something a little more exotic, such as a Z. The ASCA Web site shows pretty much every pattern imaginable (see Appendix B).

Many judges are very positive and helpful and will even give you tips when they place the class or after judging is over. Ask politely and listen carefully.

What most judges look for is a handler who can control his dog, is smooth and efficient, and emphasizes the dog's best qualities. As you can see in the photos, juniors start off young and inexperienced but quickly become smooth handlers. For example, if your dog has a very striking or pretty face, you might want to make sure that the judge has a good look at it at some point. Your dog should be very well groomed and trimmed appropriately.

Most organizations that offer conformation showing also offer Junior Showmanship. The AKC, ASCA, UKC, and CKC are just a few. 4-H offers Grooming and Handling, which is the same thing. ASCA and 4-H allow mixed breeds, but others allow only purebreds. Spayed and neutered purebreds are allowed in Junior Showmanship.

Junior Showmanship Classes

Classes for Junior Showmanship are divided by age and experience. The Novice classes are for Juniors who have not won three first places over competition. The Open classes are for experienced exhibitors, and the competition is tough.

Tricks: A Place for the Class Clown

Let's face it: The class clown is often a very clever, talented person. Dogs who star at tricks often fit that mold, too—very smart, lots of energy, and needing some direction. You may think of tricks as a sideline, but there are now even TV shows that invite talented trick dogs to come and perform for big bucks and a moment of fame. Most dogs will perform only for family picnics or at local dog events, but the rewards are still nice. Our little Lab won a $50 gift certificate to a very nice restaurant at a local Humane Society event.

So where do you start with trick training? First, look at what sort of things your dog does naturally. If she is often up on her hind legs, teaching her to dance could be easy and fun for both of you. If she likes to spin, teach her to spin and twirl on command. Those are the easy tricks!

You can then decide on additions to those tricks to make them more interesting and exciting. For example, your agility dog will probably happily jump through a hula hoop. If you add orange, red, and yellow crepe paper streamers hanging down, you now have a dog who can jump through a "hoop of fire." You are limited only by your imagination.

It is very useful to incorporate your obedience training into tricks. This will make your dog's obedience better and give you lots of options for fun tricks. A dog with a steady Sit Stay can learn to sit quietly with a biscuit on her nose. Then, when released, she will learn to toss up the biscuit and catch it—her own reward system! We must confess that many of our dogs don't catch well, so they simply drop the biscuit to the floor and then eat it.

After your dog has learned scent discrimination, you can vary the articles you use. For example, *you* can scent a $10 bill and then have someone else put out a couple of $1 bills. Your dog is so smart she will clearly pick out the bigger money! Or put out one soda can and a couple of juice cans and see whether your dog chooses healthy food or junk food.

It is also fun to add other people to the trick. You can have your dog jump over someone lying on the floor or play leapfrog with her. Someone holding his arms out in a circle can be a jump for a small to medium-sized athletic dog.

You can find great props at garage sales for next to nothing, and they add to the show. We are teaching our dogs to distinguish letters and to play basketball with a small toy hoop.

One area in which tricks really make a big impression is giving a demo for a group. Everyone from school kids to seniors in nursing homes

Balancing Work and Play

Maybe it is because tricks come with a mental picture of fun and silliness, but we find that most families practice and train harder at teaching their dogs tricks than teaching obedience. Both can be fun, so try to combine the two!

Clicker Training with Your Dog

Clicker training developed out of work done by training dolphins. It would be impossible to force a dolphin to leap and spin, but clicking the behavior got them to repeat it. Karen Pryor is recognized as one of the premier clicker trainers.

Clicker training is often the easiest way to get started on tricks. First, you need to get your dog tuned in to the clicker. Click, give a treat, and repeat. She will quickly learn that the click means something good is coming her way—think Pavlov's dogs here. You can then have a clicker with you and when your dog does something neat, click and give her a treat. She will think this over and eventually start offering behaviors so you will have more things to click. After she starts to repeat a behavior, clearly hoping for more goodies, you can name the behavior. This is a simplification, and you should check our resource lists in Appendixes A and C for good clicker training books, Web sites, and videos.

If you are a klutz and handling a clicker, treats, and your dog all at once is a bit much, you can use your voice as your clicker and keep a hand free.

loves to watch clever tricks. When you do tricks, it is obvious that both you and your dog are having fun.

There are many excellent dog trick books available (see Appendix A). Get one or two and then come up with your own variations using things your dog likes to do and any special talents she has. Search out fun and silly props to add to the performance.

Freestyle—Dance Class in a Whole New Way

Canine freestyle is another relatively new dog activity that is attracting converts all the time. Sometimes described as "dancing with dogs," freestyle can vary from elegant and intricate heelwork set to music to silly musical skits or fun tricks and moves set to music. Now, we all know every kid loves music, and most of us love to dance—even if only in secret at home. Granted, your dog does have two left feet, but undoubtedly she is a nicer dance partner than many of your friends! So put on your dancing shoes, play some fun music, grab hold of your dog, and see what fun you can have. There are currently three main organizations that deal with freestyle. All three organizations allow all dogs—mixed breeds and purebreds. WCFO is World Canine Freestyle Organization. They offer Heelwork to Music,

Musical Freestyle, and K9 Dressage divisions—all with slightly different areas of emphasis and with categories set for everyone from senior or handicapped dogs and people to junior handlers. The Canine Freestyle Federation (CFF) sticks primarily to the heelwork-to-music type performances and puts less emphasis on costumes and dance steps. The Musical Dog Sports Association (MDSA) is the newest kid on the block, and they are integrating many new ideas into their version of canine freestyle.

Classes for All Tastes

You will hear people talk about heelwork to music and musical freestyle. In heelwork to music, the movements of your dog are regulated—no jumping, no weaving. In musical freestyle, basically anything goes! This is where you will see dogs weaving between their handlers' legs or doing leaps.

Whether you intend to compete or simply plan to do demos at a local nursing home, you need to think about choreography and costumes. It can be helpful to have a friend watch while you move around with your dog to different music. Some dogs are natural country western stars, while others move best to the strong beat of rock and roll.

We try to find music that we like to listen to as well as have it match our dogs' movement. After all, you will be hearing a lot of it as you plan your routine!

Costumes can be as simple as a nice outfit and a glittery collar or a complicated affair including props such as figures to send your dog around. Each organization has different costume rules. You will get very handy at finding neat ideas at garage sales and also using hook-and-loop tape in a thousand new ways.

When starting out in freestyle, you can use many of your obedience skills. A nice heeling dog who adapts to your pace and/or the beat of the music is already halfway there. Add some turns around you like the finish after a recall, and you even have some variants. Basic moves that most dogs can quickly master are the spin or twirl—one done clockwise, one counterclockwise—weaving through your legs, side passing, and backing up. These moves can be done at your side, in front of you, or even behind you. Your imagination is the limit along with what your dog is capable of doing.

If competing on your own in the spotlight is not your idea of a fun time, there are classes for teams and pairs, or you can try to organize a local dog square-dancing team. Get some hoedown music and a good caller and adapt a few calls to dog moves, like "Sit your partner, swing around her!" and you can have a wonderful time. Plus, you know you will always have a willing partner, although we can't promise that she won't step on your feet!

For Parents Only

This chapter contains some of the most fun dog activities and some of the most frustrating. Breed and junior showmanship judging can be very subjective, and you may need to remind yourself just how perfect your dog is to *you*. We find that the performance events are much more black and white—for example, did the bar fall in agility or not? In breed, a judge may simply prefer a different color from the one your dog has. Or your dog simply may not be champion quality. That still leaves her a champion to you, though, just not to a breed organization.

In junior showmanship, we have come across wonderful judges who take their time, do a thorough job, judge the kids and not the dogs, and try to be positive and helpful. We have also run across judges who are rushed, impatient, and won't even look at a top handler unless they are also showing a lovely champion dog. It pays for both of these activities to keep notes on the individual judge and what they seemed to like or want. And then avoid them like the plague if they weren't friendly or didn't seem to like your child or your dog.

You want to avoid being "dog show parents" who nail their kids as they come out of the ring with all their faults and mistakes, or overbearing parents who groom the dog, train, etc. This is the chance for your kid to shine or fall on his own, and you are simply there to drive, pay the fees, cheer, and support. Most often your kid knows what went wrong, and he doesn't really need or appreciate hearing it from you right then and there.

If you decide that breed showing and/or junior showmanship are activities you want to pursue seriously, you will need to objectively evaluate your dog—or better yet, get an experienced person from that breed to evaluate your dog. Some dogs just aren't cut out for these activities, and rather than be frustrated, take that dog and do performance while looking for a good show prospect.

Tricks are fun, of course, and kids tend to be clever at coming up with neat ideas. Plus, as we said earlier, families tend to practice the tricks. I once taught a Household Pet class. After the first week, we added a trick of the week to each class. By the end of the session, every dog could do every trick, even though half of them were still not waiting at doors. So try to find ways to mix obedience, control, and tricks all together.

Freestyle is a blast! You need a real sense of humor, and unless you are an ex-ballerina, you need to accept that you may not be Ginger Rogers. Still, even for a nondancer, it is fun. Your dog will learn her music, and if that song comes on the radio, she may come over to get you and remind you that this is "your song." Kate did a routine to the "Tea Dance" from the *Nutcracker Suite,* and around Christmas time when it was on the radio Beep would come over to get her up to dance. Kate and I did a really fun mother/daughter routine with our Corgis (who are also mother/daughter) to the "Baby Elephant Walk," and we laughed through the whole thing.

And remember, one of the best things about tricks and freestyle is sharing the fun. Nursing homes, retirement centers, preschools, and so on all love having a group of well-trained dogs showing up to provide entertainment and excitement. And they laugh and clap just as loudly at your mistakes as at your perfect performances!

Profile: Amanda and Ripley

We met Amanda at dog shows. She works with a professional handler, as well as shows her own dogs. We most often see Amanda with her very nice Brittany, Ripley. She is always smiling and is always friendly and cheerful, whether winning or losing.

Amanda got her first dog when she was just 8 years old. Her dad had had his own dogs, but this was to be Amanda's very own dog. Her parents chose the puppy for her, and she ended up with Spencer, a male Golden Retriever.

Now, a male Golden Retriever is not the ideal dog for the average 8-year-old girl. Still, Amanda's family was supportive, and even though their young daughter was being pulled around at first by an intact, hyper male Golden, they watched her persist. Amanda says it was a sight to see! At that stage, Amanda had quite a bit of help taking care of her dog—probably even walking him.

As a teenager now, Amanda not only does all the work for her own dogs, she helps with her dad's dogs. We generally see her with her Brittany, who is a very well-behaved dog. As you can tell from the photo on page 129, Amanda is an accomplished handler.

Amanda feels that the easiest thing to train her dogs to do is tricks. She feels it is more fun and the dogs learn more quickly, probably because she isn't stressed and is having fun, too. One of the hardest things to train, in her opinion, is agility. The fast pace and quick thinking while also having to control the wild movement of a speedy sporting dog like a Golden or a Brittany make agility training difficult. Still, she enjoys her classes and hopes to compete soon.

Amanda enjoys competing with her star Brittany, Ripley.

Spencer the Golden Retriever is described by Amanda as "my heart dog. He got me started in everything I do today. He really made me the person I am. He taught me to have patience and how to let myself go and have fun!" And they have come a long way—you might see Amanda on TV, as she has earned ten firsts in Open Junior Showmanship with Ripley, and she may be competing at Westminster—a long way from the little girl being dragged by the big Golden!

For Amanda, there really are no drawbacks to having her own dogs. "I wanted them, and the responsibilities are just what comes with them. I think if you aren't ready to do everything needed for a dog, then you don't need one!" We know some adults who could use those words of wisdom.

Her love of her dogs and their strong relationship is always evident. "I can't say enough about my dogs. I love them. They are an escape from the hectic and crazy world. Really, I don't know what I would be doing if I didn't have my dogs. They are truly everything in my life and more!" And we predict that Amanda and her dogs will be in the spotlight for many years to come.

11

Civics Class: Community Service, Being a Good Neighbor, and Giving Back

These days, outrageous litigation, anti-dog legislation, and anti-dog sentiment are everywhere. Man's best friend needs to prove that he truly is a positive and contributing member of society. Some dogs do this simply by being well trained and obeying community laws such as pooper-scooper rules and leash laws. Other dogs go a step further and earn their Canine Good Citizen certificate or participate in community programs and charity fundraisers. The best thing is that virtually *every* dog is capable of all of this and can be a wonderful canine ambassador. Being a good citizen and doing your civic duty is important for you, but with your dog at your side it can even be fun!

The Canine Good Citizen Program

The Canine Good Citizen program was started by the American Kennel Club (AKC) in 1989 and has spread around the world. This is one of the few AKC programs open to all dogs, including mixed breeds. The goal of the CGC program is to encourage owners to socialize and train their dogs to the point that they are an asset to their neighborhood, not a detriment.

A dog who is a good neighbor is well behaved toward people and other dogs, making him a safer pet. These dogs are less likely to bite people or get into fights with other dogs. By going through the program, their families are proving that they are responsible dog owners. Some insurance companies even offer deals for dogs who have passed their CGC test.

There are ten basic stations or steps to the CGC program, and a dog must pass all ten successfully during one test session. Some dog clubs and shelters offer a set of training classes geared toward helping dogs train for and pass the CGC test. After a dog passes, he is recorded with the AKC and receives a certificate showing that he is a CGC.

- **Response to a friendly stranger:** The dog must greet a stranger while walking with you without being aggressive, out of control, or jumping up.
- **Sit for petting:** Again, your dog must show that he can maintain control while receiving attention from someone.
- **Appearance and grooming:** Your dog must be clean and well cared for, plus allow a stranger (mimicking a veterinarian or groomer) to touch his ears and pick up his front feet.
- **Walk on a loose leash:** This shows that your dog isn't dragging you down the street but will walk nicely with you.
- **Walk through a crowd:** This demonstrates that your dog will walk with you, ignore strangers, and behave even with other people around.
- **Sit, Down, and Stay:** Your dog needs to show that he knows how to Sit and Down, and then he has to Stay while you walk away and back (all on a long line).
- **Coming when called:** Again, done on a long line.
- **Reacting to a strange dog:** You greet a person walking her own dog, and your dog must behave.
- **Reacting to a distraction:** This could be a dropped pan, a jogger, a person with a cane—whatever—and your dog can startle but not panic or act aggressively.
- **Supervised separation:** You will hand your leash to someone and leave for three minutes—your dog has to behave, not bark or whine continuously, or fight the leash.

Signing up for a CGC class or getting the information from the AKC and training for it on your own is often the first step to a bigger addiction—competing and earning titles with your dog. We simply include this as a warning that dog training can become habit forming.

Doing Therapy Dog Work

For many dogs and families, earning the CGC is the first step on the road to becoming a certified therapy dog team. Therapy dogs are not official working dogs like search and rescue dogs, hearing dogs, or guiding eye dogs. They are well-behaved dogs, usually private pets, although sometimes resident facility dogs, who provide comfort and love to people in need. These might be hospitalized patients, seniors in retirement homes, or special-needs children. In times of stress, such as the World Trade Center destruction, therapy dogs are on hand to help comfort survivors and rescue workers.

There are two main national therapy dog groups and many local groups. All of these groups require some sort of testing for your dog. After your dog passes the test, he is given identification and set up to do visits.

Most groups use the CGC test as the basis of their testing but often add tests, as therapy dogs must be super people-proofed. An additional test your dog may be required to pass might include a "leave it" exercise, so you know he will ignore food or medicine left on the floor. Your dog must be comfortable around equipment like IV stands, walkers, crutches, and wheelchairs. And he must be outgoing enough to reach out to people who may not be able to reach for him or talk to him. Some dogs simply have no interest in people other than their own families. They may be great demo dogs, but they aren't the best therapy dogs.

Therapy dog organizations provide insurance coverage for you and your dog while you're working as a pet therapist. This is a very nice feature that makes some facilities feel more comfortable about allowing dogs in to visit with residents.

Therapy dogs need health screening, too. They must be free of parasites or any health problems that they might spread to a patient. Good grooming is essential—your dog should be bathed, be free of any infections or sores, and have nails trimmed ahead of time and filed so they aren't sharp. You want your dog to look his best, as you are hoping to brighten up someone's day!

A special group of therapy dogs is involved in helping children learn to read better. Studies have shown that children advance more quickly reading

Therapy Dog Organizations

The two main therapy dog organizations are Therapy Dog International (TDI) and the Delta Society. TDI sticks strictly to therapy dogs, but Delta Society has programs for a wide range of assistance dogs. For Delta work, *you* may need to take a test as well. See Appendix B to locate information.

aloud to a dog than to a human volunteer. Dogs are not at all judgmental, never criticize, and appear genuinely interested in the stories being read—no matter what the topic and even if they have heard that book a thousand times before. Of course, the dogs love the attention, and the children love having an audience. One of the first groups to do this was a group out west called the Intermountain Therapy Animal Group. Their R.E.A.D. program, for Reading Education Assistance Dogs, has been the basis for many programs. See Appendix B for further information.

Walking a Walkathon

Walkathons are a great way to show support for your community. The best part is that many times your dog can come, too. Most walkathons are for nonprofit organizations that provide all sorts of services for your community, be it cancer research or seeing eye dog training. Local shelters sometimes hold walkathons to earn money to help feed the animals at the shelter and expand so that they can take in even more. As the photo shows, your whole family can get involved.

Most walkathons require a minimum entry fee. All you have to do is contact the group sponsoring the walkathon and ask for a sponsor form. Then try to collect as many donations as you can, asking friends, family, and even teachers. Every cent counts, so don't turn down your best friend's nickel! This money is then turned in to the organization on the date of the walkathon, and you get to go with your dog. Often, walkathons have corporate sponsors who donate T-shirts or goody bags to the walkers.

Your whole family can take part in walkathons!

Costume classes are popular fundraisers.

Dog and pet-related walkathons often offer trick and costume classes at the conclusion of the walkathon with prizes donated by local stores. The photo shows a cute costume idea. Some even hold potluck dinners, and the food is always good!

Not all walkathons will allow dogs to accompany you, so be sure to check. Usually if your dog is well behaved, has a current rabies vaccination, and is licensed, there won't be any problems. Still, it is important to check first, in case certain neighborhoods don't want dogs walking through. Some walkathons are so big they need to shuttle people to the starting points. Sometimes the busses won't allow dogs, so you may have to walk a bit extra.

Always take your dog's needs into consideration. If the walk is in the winter on city streets, you may need to be careful about road salt on his paws. No matter when the walk is held, you should plan on carrying water for your dog and a bowl for him to drink from—collapsible bowls are great for this. And, remember, your dog can carry his own supplies in his backpack!

Working at Dog Events

When you go to a show, look around. You'll notice that there are a million people racing around doing all sorts of things. Dog events require lots of people to be run efficiently, and believe it or not, volunteers often make the difference. It is only fair to give back to the sports that offer you and your dog so much. One real benefit is that volunteers often get excellent ringside seats and may get to interact with the judges. From assisting, you may learn what judges are looking for and get hints to help improve your own performance.

Agility trials require the most volunteer help. Each class needs a ring crew to set bars and fix equipment, a gate steward to get dogs on the line in the right order, a leash runner to shuttle each lead from the start line to the finish line, a score sheet runner to ferry score sheets from the scribe to the score table, a timer to time each run, and a scribe to record faults. That's a lot of jobs! Offer to take a job for one of the classes you aren't competing in. Agility people tend to be very nice and are always willing to teach you how to do a particular job or show you where to go. And it's worth the effort—workers usually get free lunch as well as tickets for a worker-only raffle. Some trials even offer free T-shirts!

The main volunteer job for obedience is stewarding. Each ring needs stewards to be posts for the figure 8 as well as several other jobs. If you are assigned to a utility ring, you may have to put out gloves and articles. Both open and utility events have jumps that need to be set as well. After you've done a lot of stewarding, you may be chosen to work the score table, an honor reserved for the highest quality stewards. Many clubs pay their stewards anywhere from $5 to $50 or offer free lunch and snacks.

Herding trials need scribes and timers. The scribe writes down everything the judge says about a run, and the timer times the run from start to finish. If you are experienced with handling livestock, you may be asked to help with stock *set out*. Even inexperienced kids can help carry out crates of ducks to the outrun location.

Carting dogs can participate in walkathons, help with fundraisers, and deliver drinks and supplies as volunteers.

Conformation shows have stewards, too, but usually they prefer registered stewards or people with a lot of experience at shows. If you decide you want to steward for conformation, volunteer at a local match to get some experience.

Volunteering has lots of benefits. You might get paid or at least get free food—always a good thing for kids! Many clubs hold special worker raffles. Each time you help out, you get a ticket to put in for that special raffle. Prizes might even include free entry at the next trial!

If your school requires community service or volunteer work, your dog activities can count. You also gain positive work experiences to put on your 4-H records, job resume, and college applications. Plus, involving your dog makes it more fun for everyone, as the photo on page 136 shows.

While volunteering, you will work with and meet people from all walks of life, all of whom share a common interest with you—dogs. Another great bonus to volunteering at an event is that you can watch and learn the whole time you are helping. In agility, getting to watch some of the top handlers and their dogs from your excellent vantage point as a bar setter is a real education.

Helping Out at the Humane Society

Most Humane Societies and animal shelters are understaffed and overworked. Many of them count on unpaid volunteers to help out—especially with the extras like grooming, walking, and socializing the dogs. You can even help increase adoptions by training basic obedience commands like Sit, Down, Stay, and Come. Due to insurance considerations, many shelters can allow only volunteers of a certain age—such as above 14 years of age. Age requirements vary in different locales, so check to be sure.

If you do go and volunteer at a shelter, remember that you are there as a support person. You will probably not be included in decision making, and sometimes you may feel upset with shelter policies. You have to remember that most shelters are doing the best they can with minimal budgets and manpower. Follow directions carefully, as safety is often a consideration in drawing up guidelines. Always think about the possibility of spreading disease from one dog to another and how to prevent that.

If you are too young to volunteer in a shelter or feel it is just too overwhelming for you, you can still help by doing fundraising or collecting donations for a group. You can make dog treats or clever dog crafts (see chapter 13) and sell these yourself or bring them to the shelter gift shop. Encourage your school class to choose a shelter to support as a class project.

If the shelter has a walkathon as a fundraiser, encourage all your friends to get pledges and walk with you. A group of enthusiastic kids *can* make a difference!

Getting Political: Pushing Papers for Power

You can also help dogdom by writing letters and working to push for legislation that will help dogs. For example, banning certain dog breeds really doesn't make much sense. It would be much better to ban individual dogs who are dangerous—we all know pit bulls who are sweet dogs and Chihuahuas who are tiny sharks. Very often it is the irresponsible owner who ought to be banned!

You could help take petitions around or even work to develop responsible dog-owning guidelines for your community, such as leash laws. Kids from our 4-H club have helped to create a dog park in one city and work for shelters in our community.

Although many political groups aren't into having kids help with petitions, they will happily take your labor stuffing envelopes and folding papers. You might get drafted to help operate a booth at a community event or hand out petitions at a dog show. Working and listening to the discussions can be an education in itself. Shelters and foundations such as service dog training groups often have mailings to organize. An extra set of hands (or in the case of our 4-H group, sixteen sets of hands) makes a tedious job go quickly and earns you respect and thanks.

Becoming a Foster Parent

If your family isn't quite ready for a full-time dog, but you would enjoy some canine companionship, you may want to look into volunteering to be a foster parent for a rescue group or a shelter. As a foster parent, you agree to care for a dog for a short time while the dog adjusts to real life, as in the case of ex-racer Greyhounds, or to help a purebred dog who has been left at a shelter adapt back to being in a home. Sometimes foster homes simply help with space crunches at a shelter, freeing up a space for another homeless dog.

Fostering requires a special team—people who are willing to give a lot of love and effort over a short period of time to help a dog in need. You may have to work through some behavior problems, add some basic training, or

Alternative Ways to Help with Foster Work

Some dogs are not happy about sharing their home with other dogs. You need to be sure that your dog is mentally comfortable with strange dogs visiting and give him extra time and attention. If he just isn't willing to peacefully allow another dog in the house, then offer other skills, such as driving a dog to his new home via the Canine Underground Railroad.

simply provide love to a worried dog. Many foster parents end up falling in love and keeping at least one foster dog, but ideally you help the foster dog find a new forever home so that you can help another dog in dire straits.

Our Fostering Experience

We fostered a lovely young Belgian Tervuren for about six weeks. She then left our family to join her forever home. We delivered her halfway to Connecticut, and we still think of her any time we drive by the "hand-over" spot. You do leave a piece of your heart with each foster dog.

Some groups can provide financial assistance for foster dogs (for food and grooming), but other groups are so financially strapped that they hope you can kick in some funds, too. Make sure you know all the details before you approach your parents.

Purebred rescue groups try to provide lots of backup and support for their foster parents. Often, they have better funding and a more experienced support group than some shelters do. That could mean financial aid to help with food and veterinary costs or simply guidance over the phone on how to stop your wonderful foster dog from ripping open the sofa. In return, it is hoped that you can provide a fairly accurate idea of the temperament and activity level of the dog in question. Learning what training skills the dog has will also help the rescue group in checking out potential adopters to find the best match.

When fostering a shelter dog, you may be expected to chip in more for expenses, as most shelters are already on a tight budget. Any insights into the dog in your care and any additional training you can provide to make him more adoptable are all benefits to the shelter.

It can be difficult when the time comes to hand over your foster dog, but you can feel good about helping this canine in a time of trouble and guiding him to a new life. The phone calls, letters, and photos you receive telling you how wonderful he is and how well he fits in are part of your reward.

Raising an Assistance Dog

If your family would love to give back, literally in this case, you might want to look into raising a puppy for a service dog group. In this case, you take an 8-week-old pup, often a Labrador Retriever, although other breeds are used, and raise him until he is between 12 and 18 months of age, depending on the program. The organization will help you out with classes to teach the pup his basic commands and provide guidance as to care. Some groups help out with veterinary and food costs, but others may expect you to donate those expenses.

What your family is doing is giving this pup the absolute best start in life to help him in his future as a working dog. You will socialize him, take him to a wide variety of places and expose him to the many everyday things a dog will encounter. Your puppy will wear a special cape or bandana identifying him as a service dog puppy, and this gives him special access rights so he can even go into stores and restaurants with you. He can lie quietly by your table in a restaurant and even go to the movie theater. It is important that he learn how to behave in these places so that when he is placed with his special-needs person, he will already know what to do. The hard part is that at the end of his time with you, you must return the pup to the organization for specialized training and placement with his new person. Still, your sadness will be balanced by your joy at seeing how much he adds to someone else's life. If your pup doesn't make it as a service dog—perhaps he is too friendly or has trouble concentrating on his work—you may be given the option of adopting him as a permanent member of your family. Still, you hope that he is the star of his graduating class and not a dog who needs a different job in life.

These service dogs may be trained to assist a deaf or blind person or to help someone confined to a wheelchair by operating lights, carrying objects, picking up objects, and sometimes even helping to pull the wheelchair. Their talents are amazing, and the difference they can make in helping a person become more independent is astounding!

For Parents Only

This chapter is near and dear to my heart. Working with our dogs to help make the world a brighter place is one of the neatest things we do with our dogs. Both my children did their first nursing home visits in strollers at 6 weeks of age, accompanying at least one of our dogs and often our cat, too. Both kids are tolerant of people with handicaps and special needs and of all ages. They realize how lucky they are and want to share some of their good fortune with others.

There is no end to the good works your family and dogs can do. Using the dogs makes it more fun, and it is wonderful to include them in your activities. Still, there will be some dogs who are just not comfortable with public service activities, so you have to evaluate your dog objectively—or have someone else do it for you. If your dog or you are not comfortable doing visits, then look into walkathons, volunteering at your shelter, or fostering.

I feel it is important that my children know how lucky they are and that they start while still young learning about giving back to their community. My 4-H group makes community service a requirement, and scouting and school groups stress giving back, too. Your child is already a responsible caring person due to the influence of having a dog, so take advantage of that and spread the wealth!

Profile: Hunter and Smudge

For Hunter, dogs were simply a way of life. Having an Australian Shepherd breeder for a mom meant he was exposed to dogs from day one. And this gregarious redhead loved being with the dogs, going to dog shows, and looking forward to showing himself.

Then tragedy struck. At just 5 years of age, Hunter was diagnosed with Wilms tumor. His was an aggressive version, and he was to battle it just as aggressively for the next eight years, including two stem cell transplants, surgeries, and chemotherapy.

Through it all, Hunter knew he could rely on his dogs and his dog friends. The prospect of going to shows and agility trials and getting to see his many friends as well as compete helped Hunter focus on healing and staying well. His was a life of treatments, remissions, and resurgence of his cancer. Despite his treatments, Hunter continued to compete with Smudge in agility, as shown in the photo. His dogs kept him company in the dark hours of pain and sadness and rejoiced with him during remissions. They were his 24-hour guardians and his nonstop caretakers. For one blessed 32-month period, Hunter felt great, and everyone hoped his cancer had at last admitted defeat.

Hunter and Smudge were a winning agility team.

The dog community rallied around Hunter, organizing financial assistance for his family, arranging fun outings, and providing shoulders to lean on when they needed them. Take the Lead is a dog organization that exists to help members of the dog community when they have problems. They were one of many groups that assisted Hunter's family.

Unfortunately, Hunter's tumors returned with a vengeance. The return of this devastating problem in January 2003 was to signal the beginning of Hunter's last fight. Still, Hunter managed to show his Australian Shepherd Kodak at the March shows in Syracuse, New York, and see his many dog show friends.

As June waned and July approached, it was clear Hunter was losing the battle to stay on earth. All this time, his faithful Australian

Shepherd, Smudge, Eddtide's Just a Smudge NA NAJ, was there for Hunter. Together, they had earned agility titles, had been chosen as the Best Junior Handler Team at the Australian Shepherd National, and simply had been best buddies. As you can see in the photo, Hunter and Smudge truly were best buddies.

On July 17, 2003, Hunter made a tape for his friends and family. His faithful Smudge lay by his side. "I wish I could breathe like her. . . . I'm sorry, Smudge. I wish I could go out there and run and help with you, too, out in the woods and fields, just being with you and showing you at dog shows. I miss you, and I love you. . . . [Smile] Smudge is a blessing from God to me." On July 21, 2003, Hunter left us.

Hunter and Smudge were constant companions.

Although his life was short, Hunter influenced many people, especially in the dog world. There is an agility ring dedicated to him at the Over Rover facility in Cato, New York, and we all think of him whenever we go there. At the ASCA shows in July, memorial fireworks, sparklers, and readings are dedicated to Hunter. He loved his Aussies, and through them and because of them, his world was a better place.

12

Field Trips: Traveling with Your Dog

Just as we all look forward to field trips as a way of getting out of school, traveling with your dog is great fun, too. Whether you and your dog are competing in agility, working toward your championship, or investigating a new park, traveling requires a lot of planning and organizing. Discussing which one of you gets the bed and who sleeps on the floor alone can take quite a long time. With luck, you can even include your dog in your vacation plans. If you've done your homework and your dog is well trained and well socialized, he will be welcome in many places and on many trips.

Safety in the Car

We've all seen it: a big guy cruising around town in his rusty pickup truck with a Rottweiler in the back sticking her head out to catch the breeze. *No!* Each year, many dogs die as a result of falling or jumping from pickup trucks. They may get hit by the car traveling behind or run off and get lost. Some communities actually have laws preventing animals from riding loose in the back of a pickup. You can safely tie down a crate or arrange for a seat belt option, but even so, remember that you need to consider the temperature and weather. Your dog won't be comfortable in hot sun or in cold rain or snow. A cap on the truck bed is a help, but you still need to consider the conditions.

If your dog is riding inside the car, it is not a good idea to let her put her head out the window—although it may look like fun. For one thing, dogs

A crate is a safe option for your dog in the car—obviously close the doors first!

can get ear, eye, and nose infections from debris blowing off the road. So keep the window shut! As for inside the car, there are several means of keeping your dog's ride safe and happy.

Having a crate in the car is a good idea if you are going to be traveling a lot. This way, your dog is in a safe place where she can't get into trouble while you visit the restroom or eat lunch. If you have a puppy or young dog, the crate will prevent her from chewing anything and prevent any accidents from spreading all over the car. Crates are also nice because you can stack things on top of them, which can be useful if you have a lot of baggage. Crates are available in pretty colors, too.

The crate should have a comfortable blanket or bedding of some type in it, along with a water bowl so your dog can sip water or lick at ice. You might want to add a toy or a chew item, but make sure that there is room left for your dog!

Carsickness can be a problem for some dogs. The crate is helpful here, as she won't be throwing up on your nice upholstered car seats. You can talk to your veterinarian about motion sickness medications such as Dramamine or try using the natural root ginger. Even gingersnap cookies might help; if not, the whole family can enjoy them anyway.

If you don't want your dog to ride in a crate, doggie seat belts and barriers are also available. Seat belts come in many sizes. Basically, they are harnesses that attach to the regular seat belt so that your dog is strapped in.

Seat belts are best for older, calmer dogs, as the young ones can get excited and tangle themselves up. The photo shows an older dog who is comfortable wearing her seat belt. Worse still, some dogs might try to chew through the harness and escape. Be sure not to leave your dog alone in the car with the seat belt on. Seat belts can work very well if you have a three-person backseat and two kids. Your dog won't even fuss about having to be in the middle and not getting her own window.

A seat belt can be another safe travel option.

Barriers tend to be one size fits all. These are usually plastic or metal bars that can be placed behind the seats of your car so that your dog can't climb up into your lap or get in the way. This way, your dog can still be loose in the car but won't accidentally cause an accident (no pun intended). One concern here is that if the barrier blocks off the back of your car and you need to open the back door to get your dog out, you have to be careful that she doesn't leap out and run off. Training a consistent Wait from puppyhood is important here.

Although the safety of your dog is a top concern, the safety of everyone in the car is important, too. If your dog is riding loose, not only may she get badly hurt in an accident if she gets thrown about, but she can crash into and injure people in the car. A loose dog can escape from your car in a crash and run off or get hit by traffic. Being in a crate has saved the lives of many dogs involved in car accidents.

Flying High—Taking to the Skies

Ideally, you should avoid flying with your dog unless you have to. Small dogs and puppies can fly in small carriers placed under the seat—basically soft, collapsible crates. Most airlines will allow one or two pets in the cabin

Weather Warning

Although you may know this, it doesn't hurt to repeat it—*do not* leave your dog in the car in hot weather. Even with a window cracked and the car parked in the shade, the heat will build up quickly. Remember, shade moves over the day. So, on hot days, leave your dog at home in the luxury of air conditioning, or at least her own fan!

First or Third Class?

Kate's puppy Queezle flew from Oregon to New York in a carrier, accompanying Kate. Her littermate had to ride in cargo in a crate, but both girls handled the trip well. Queezle especially liked being carried through the airports with her little head poking out of the top of her bag.

on a flight. You need to make sure they will accept your dog and that you fill out all of the proper paperwork and carry it with you. A rabies certificate is always required, and some airlines may want health certificates as well—even for dogs in the cabin.

True service dogs such as dogs who assist blind or deaf people are allowed by law to ride in the cabin and can lie down quietly at their person's feet. Other large dogs must ride in cargo.

Dogs are put into a special pressurized section of the cargo compartment. The crate your dog travels in must meet a number of airline requirements, including size and construction. You need to check with your individual airline for their specifications. Health records such as a rabies certificate and a health certificate will need to be attached to the crate, along with food and water if the trip will be very long. Try to avoid tranquilizers if possible. You want your dog to be alert to pant or shiver if she needs to in certain temperatures and to bark loudly if her crate gets forgotten in a baggage area.

The flight certificates ask whether the dog has been acclimated to certain temperatures and can handle them. Most airlines will not fly dogs if the temperature is too high. So, in summer, you may need to book flights at night. Try to arrange for nonstop flights if at all possible, as you don't want your dog becoming lost luggage!

It is a good idea to put plenty of shredded, absorbent bedding in the crate in case your dog has an accident. A chew item may keep her calm and happy. And ice cubes are better than water in a bowl if you feel she will need a drink. They will melt slowly, and she won't spill water all over and end up wet and uncomfortable.

Preparing for the Flight

If you do need to fly with your dog, take some positive actions. Book nonstop flights if possible. Accustom your dog to a crate if she isn't already used to one. Stay with her as long as possible up until loading, and make sure all the airline personnel know there is a dog on board.

What to Pack

On trips, your dog needs the same services she gets at home. Be sure to pack everything you might need. Here is a list of things that you should always take with you.

- Leash
- Poop bags
- Dog food
- Bed blankets
- Water
- Bowls
- Toys
- Chew items
- Pet identification/tags (even if your dog is microchipped or tattooed)
- Any medications
- Medical records, including rabies certificates

Hotel Etiquette

For long trips, you may need to stay in a hotel. If you make reservations ahead of time (and we highly recommend doing this when traveling with your dog), be sure to find out whether the hotel allows dogs. If not, *do not* try to sneak your dog in anyway. This is strongly frowned upon and can result in you being banned from certain hotels. Other hotels may have limits on the size of dog they accept or charge an additional pet fee.

If you have a puppy in the hotel room, bring a crate for her to stay in. This way, there is no risk of anything getting chewed or damaged, and she won't soil the rug. An alternative is to keep her in the bathroom, although you should check to make sure there is nothing she can chew. Also, use a barrier of some sort rather than closing the door. If she starts to cry in the night, you want to be able to hear her and respond before your neighbors do.

No matter how old your dog is, don't leave her unattended in the room for long periods of time. Some dogs bark when they get lonely or start chewing out of boredom or stress from being in a new place. Also be sure to clean up after your dog. This will help ensure that the hotel will continue to allow dogs. Another good idea is to put your own sheets or comforters on the beds. These will help reduce the amount of hair on the bedspread and protect the bed from muddy paws. Try to keep your dog quiet in the halls and always leave a tip for the cleaning staff.

We suggest that you always pack a regular leash as well as a retractable one. Retractable leashes are great for walking your dog in parks, letting her run a bit, and maybe even for a short game of fetch. However, they are very dangerous around buildings—your dog can get around a corner, and you don't know who or what is there. A retractable leash cord can dig right into flesh and do some damage if you or someone else gets tangled in it. Some parks now outlaw these leashes.

Campground Etiquette

Camping offers more freedom than staying in a hotel, but many of the same rules still apply. Your dog should not be running loose around the campground. You need to diligently pick up after her and keep her confined or with you on leash. No barking at late hours, and she should be in your camper, RV, or tent with you. Remember her creature comforts, too—a comfortable, dry bed is important for her as well as you.

If you are hiking to a campsite, your dog can carry many, if not all, of her own supplies in a backpack. If she is a medium-sized or large dog, she might even consent to carry some of your things! Even out in the wilderness, many forest and park areas require dogs to be on leash. This is for their own safety as well as common courtesy for other hikers. You don't want your dog scaring other hikers or running off and irritating a bear, which would scare all of you and could lead to someone being hurt.

The Social Dog

When you travel with your dog, you really see why it was so important to do all that early socialization and training. A well-trained dog is welcome in many places. She will lie quietly under your sidewalk café table, whether in Boston or Paris. She will walk at your side through crowds and not jump on people or bark or growl. You won't be dragged across busy city streets or cause a commotion flying along crowded sidewalks. She will Sit or Down Stay while you write out checks so your handwriting will be somewhat legible.

A well-behaved dog will be welcome in the houses of friends you stay with, saving you hotel bills. She will tolerate other dogs and behave around other pets—even unusual ones like birds or reptiles. However, we are *not* recommending that you leave your Labrador Retriever alone with your host's parrot!

In return, your dog will provide you with company and security on your trips. No one will break into your hotel room after one loud bark. You will be safe unloading your car at night in a parking lot. (One of our Belgian Tervurens prevented a mugging in a parking lot late one night.) Your dog will also let you choose whatever CD you want to play without fussing or let you change the radio station as much as you want. She won't ask "Are we there yet?" although she will need bathroom breaks. Her bathrooms breaks will force you to stop and stretch your legs, too.

Boarding—Kennel, That Is, Not School!

There will be times when your dog will not be able to travel with you. For those times, a good boarding kennel can be an excellent solution.

Try to check out kennels *before* you need one! Most kennels allow tours, but don't show up at the crack of dawn. Kennel staff need time to clean, feed, and exercise their boarders. Then they can give tours!

Ideally, a kennel would be very small and homey with lots of extra attention and no runs or crates in sight. That is not very realistic, however. For sanitation reasons, most kennels have runs of tile, asphalt, or cement that can be easily cleaned and disinfected. For smaller dogs, large stainless steel crates may be appropriate. Dogs should have fresh water available at all times—either in stainless steel bowls or automatic waterers.

Many kennels will let you bring your own food—a necessity if your dog is on a special diet. Also be sure to pack any medications she may be on. Most kennels will charge an extra fee for medicating your dog.

Ask about exercise. Some kennels have large runs, but others use staff to walk pets. You might want to arrange an extra walk or play time for an energetic young dog. For safety's sake, your dog will need to be in a securely fenced area or on a leash.

Look to see that comfortable bedding is available, especially if your dog is a senior citizen. You may be able to bring your own blankets, beds, or at least a toy or two for your dog to enjoy the scents of home. Do realize that your

Choosing a Kennel

Here's what to look for in a kennel:

- Lack of odors
- No stool (other than fresh) in runs
- Plenty of good ventilation
- Clean water available 24/7
- Nice beds (or ask if you can bring one from home)
- Safety features such as double fencing
- Dogs who seem basically happy

bedding and toys may get dirty, or that your dog may chew them. So don't leave great-aunt Beth's special knitted afghan for your dog to sleep on.

During your tour, realize that many dogs may be barking or upset simply because they see a new person (that's you) walking through. Many kennels play quiet background music to soothe dogs—remember that saying about how "music soothes the savage beast." The kennel staff should know the dogs by name and genuinely seem to like dogs.

If you have two dogs, think long and hard about whether they will be happy boarding together or would do best with separate but adjoining kennels. Two young rowdy dogs might enjoy being together to wrestle and play, but an older dog might like some peace and quiet.

The kennel may have specific requirements in the way of health care—they may want a canine or kennel cough vaccine given before boarding. Be sure to leave information on how to reach you and your veterinarian. Bring a copy of your dog's vaccination records when you drop her off. You may want to request a bath on the day you pick your dog up. Even the cleanest of kennels may still have a slight disinfectant odor.

Don't make a huge production when you leave your dog. That will only make her more anxious and upset. Be upbeat, giver her a quick pat, and off you go. While most dogs look longingly after you, they usually turn and go off quite cheerfully with their new kennel staff friend, and some dogs seem to enjoy meeting new dog friends.

Baby (Pet) Sitter—Another Great Option

If you have more than one dog, or even just one, a pet sitter can be a wonderful option. A pet sitter comes to your house to take care of your dog and other pets (see Appendix B). Different arrangements can be made—a pet sitter may stop by three times a day to walk your dog, feed her, groom her, and play with her, or she may stay at your house.

There are professional pet sitting organizations, or you can look around your neighborhood for a trusted friend. This is an ideal situation in that your dog is less stressed as she is in her own house, lying on her own bed, and running in her own yard. Still, it is important that the pet sitter knows how to recognize any problems and is extremely conscientious.

You will need to be very thorough in writing out your dog's care and her normal routine. If her last walk at night is usually 9 P.M., having a last walk at 8 P.M. could lead to accidents. Make sure that adequate food and any medications are at home and that directions for feeding and medicating are clear. A pet sitter should only walk your dog on leash or stay with her in your fenced yard. Your dog should meet your pet sitter if that person is someone she

For Parents Only

At first, the thought of adding your dog to your vacation plans may seem overwhelming, but it can work out. Obviously, if your ideal trip is to fly to Paris and spend four days haunting the Louvre, it might be best to leave your dog at home in a kennel or with a pet sitter. Still, if your family camps, likes to hike, or is heading for the beach, you may be able to bring your dog along.

Always check ahead to be sure your dog is welcome in your hotel. Most campgrounds do allow dogs, but we recommend you check with them, too. Many large tourist attractions have short-term kennels on site so that your dog can safely recline in temperature-controlled comfort while you enjoy the amusement park. Always check ahead, as you don't want to leave your dog in the car in warm weather.

Having a dog along will open up new vistas for you. Dogs seem to be natural magnets for animal lovers, and you may meet some new friends. Walking your dog may lead you to discover new parks and places. We have had fun hiking parts of the Appalachian Trail and going through corn mazes with our dogs.

Although it may be hard, there are times when it is best for your dog to remain at home. Dogs do love running on the beach, but if it is very hot, her feet will burn on the sand, and you will need to provide shade and water for her. Some beaches have areas closed off due to nesting shore birds. If your dog gets carsick and will need to be left alone in a room or cabin for long hours every day, she is probably better off in a quality kennel back at home.

Likewise, a dog who is not comfortable with a lot of traffic and commotion won't be comfortable even in a penthouse suite in the city. Although we know how hard it can be to go off and leave your beloved companion at home, sometimes it truly is the best thing for her.

doesn't know, before you head off on a weeklong trip. You need to be sure both your dog and the pet sitter are comfortable with each other.

An excellent source of knowledgeable pet sitters can be assistants at your dog's groomer or veterinary technicians from your dog's vet clinic. These are people who know dogs and, just as important, know *your* dog, so she won't be left with a stranger.

One additional plus to having a pet sitter is that she can care for all your pets, including fish, cats, and birds, and even your plants! We have horses, donkeys, sheep, ducks, and a goat as well as house pets, so a pet sitter is the ideal—maybe only—solution for us!

Profile: Matt and BooBoo

BooBoo is a very cute spaniel mix—only about 14 inches high but with enough energy and spirit for a dog five times her size. Matt was only 7 years old when BooBoo entered his life as a very special Christmas present. Matt's parents chose the adult dog—BooBoo was about 2 years old at the time—at the local shelter because they felt her energy level matched Matt's. BooBoo was lucky, as many people would have walked by the cute but adult dog. However, what better choice for a hyper boy than a hyper dog?

Right from the start, Matt has handled most of BooBoo's care. He was lucky to miss out on all those early-morning walks since BooBoo was beyond puppyhood! BooBoo has been an easy dog for Matt to train and work with. She is very smart and learned "shake" right away. Since she is such a busy, energetic dog, the hardest thing for BooBoo has been learning the Down Stay. Even now, she pops up sometimes.

Matt feels that the only drawback to having a dog of his own is sometimes just not having a lot of time. Caring for BooBoo does take time, and Matt wishes he had more time to do things with her. BooBoo has shown great talent in agility and has competed at the New York State Fair in agility with Matt. Because of BooBoo, Matt got involved with 4-H and has won a County Medal Award.

Matt and BooBoo are similar in many ways and always best of friends!

Matt says, "Boo is by far my very best friend. She is someone who is always around for me and keeps me company no matter what." Matt likes to work on cars and trucks—he is already a good mechanic at just 14 years old—and Boo likes to supervise his work. While BooBoo and Matt may not look a lot alike, as you can see in the photo, they are similar in many ways. To Matt, BooBoo is his buddy, his best friend, and his partner—helping him and keeping him company.

For Matt, BooBoo is one of the most valuable things in his life. “Boo is the one I care the most about—she is very special to me.”

People say that dogs are like their people and vice versa, often citing physical characteristics. Matt feels that he and BooBoo are very similar in that they both like to pull pranks and occasionally cause some trouble.

13

Fine Arts, Home Economics, and Shop Class

For a cold or rainy day when you and your dog just don't feel like braving the weather, there are plenty of other things to do. If you enjoy making things with your hands or cooking, be it for you or your dog, the possibilities are endless! The items mentioned here can be made as gifts, for donations to your local shelter or rescue group, or as fundraisers for any group with which you are associated.

There are many different crafts that you can make for or relating to your dog. Homemade crafts also make excellent Christmas gifts, and you can even make some training equipment for your dog. If you're in 4-H, you can enter your crafts at your local fair, earning both premiums and fame.

Rubber Stamping

One of our favorite types of crafting is rubber stamping. Rubber stamps come in all shapes and sizes and can be found with any breed of dog or design you can imagine. The best thing about stamps is that they can be reused and stay good for a long time. Many rubber stamps are beautiful renditions of different dog breeds or dog equipment (see Appendix D). Our 4-H club makes many different crafts such as zipper pulls, magnets, and stationery that we sell as fundraisers for our club.

Zipper pulls are fun and easy to make and work well as fundraisers.

Zipper pulls make great gifts. All you need is some shrink plastic that can be found at a local craft store and permanent or archival ink. Just stamp the plastic and cut out each shape, leaving enough room to punch a hole in the top. Punch the hole before baking. Then follow the instructions on the package for baking the plastic. When the plastic cools, all you have to do is slip a lanyard through the hole, and you have your very own zipper pull! You may even want to color the stamped plastic before you bake it for extra eye-catching appeal. We have used markers, gel pens, and colored pencils with success. As you can see in the photo, these zipper pulls make cute and unique craft items.

Stationery is always useful, and many people love to get or send cards showing off their favorite breed of dog or any dog theme. There are even stamps with dog-themed quotes such as "Sealed with dog slobber." Buying card stock in bulk lets you make up cards, postcards, and envelopes very inexpensively. To stamp on paper, you don't need the special inks, so you have access to more colors. You can even create a whole scene with other stamps such as sheep for a herding scene.

Bookmarks are another easy-to-make item. You can stamp a sheet of cardstock to make many bookmarks. Then laminate the sheet and cut out the individual bookmarks. You may even want to punch a hole at one end and create a tassel or braid yarn to make a tail.

Just as with shrink plastic, whenever you stamp on wood, you should use permanent or archival ink. This ink won't run or smear if it gets wet. You can find all sorts of wooden things in a craft store, from hearts to boxes to picture frames. The wooden boxes shown here are very popular. For some crafts, you might want to paint the wood first and then stamp it, but for others you can just stamp the unpainted wood. Let the ink dry overnight and then varnish it to help preserve the wood.

With flat wooden cutouts, you can stick special magnet tape onto the back to create a personalized magnet. Some craft stores sell hooks to add or have hangers such as twine already attached to basic shapes.

The Angel Policy

Many rubber stamp companies and artists have an angel policy. This means that you may sell items that you hand stamp with their product. You may not, however, make reproductions, such as stamping one card and then xeroxing it.

Stamping on wood can make nice gifts.

Another easy rubber stamp craft is to make magnets by stamping on magnetic paper. You can order this paper from craft suppliers. Just stamp the paper using the archival ink. You must let the ink dry thoroughly—this may take a day or two. Then spray the magnet paper with a clear acrylic spray. When that is dry, and it dries quickly, you can cut out the magnets. Using special edging scissors with different shapes makes your magnets even more unique. We have even been able to find the magnetic paper in color, so you can do different colors for different holidays, such as orange for Halloween and red and green for Christmas.

Rubber stamping can be done on fabric as well. Again, you need special ink and should try stamping a small piece of fabric first to be sure the texture will work with the stamps. Many rubber stamps are detailed works of art, and the exquisite detail may be lost when stamping on fabric. Still, bandanas, T-shirts, and tote bags can all be stamped very nicely. Special techniques can be used to stamp on velvet as well—using not ink, but rather the impression of the rubber stamp.

Sewing

If you like to sew, you might want to try your hand at making toys, beds, or even clothing for your dog. If you think sewing is for sissies, think again. You can pretend you are practicing for when you are a world-famous surgeon and are suturing up the president after saving his life. If nothing else, you can do "toy surgery" periodically and stitch back together the toys your dog has enjoyed taking apart.

Fleece and fake fur are very popular for dog toys as they are fuzzy and fun for dogs to chew on. For a simple toy, all you have to do is cut out two identical pieces of fabric in whatever shape you choose. Then sew about three-quarters of the way around the toy, leaving an opening. This opening is for you to put stuffing and squeakers inside (see Appendix D). Polyester stuffing can be bought in bulk and is considered child safe, so we figure it is dog safe, too. After the toy is stuffed to your satisfaction, sew the opening shut and present it to your dog! If you want a more challenging design, there are patterns available, or you can even make up your own.

Dog beds are fairly similar to make, although you have several options as to what you stuff them with. Stuffing makes for a nice, poofy bed, but if your dog is a Saint Bernard, you may not want to buy that much stuffing! Another option is to buy a pillow and cover it with fleece or a fake fur pillowcase. You can put a zipper on one end or even leave an end open for easy cleaning. Carpet foam also works quite well as a filler —it comes in different thicknesses and is fairly inexpensive.

If you want to make clothing for your dog, pay a visit to your local craft or fabric store. You should be able to find all sorts of different patterns featuring everything from doggie raincoats to fleece jackets and beyond. To keep costs down, watch for sales, save coupons, and check out the remnant

You can make fun costumes for your dog for every holiday and season!

section. A small piece of pretty fleece might make a small dog bed or a number of dog toys. Costumes for dogs can be fun, too, as shown in the photo on page 158.

Appendix D shares the name of a site that sells fabric showing almost every breed of dog. You can buy the fabric as well as already-sewn items. With the fabric, your imagination is your limit as you come up with neat ideas for you, your house, or your dog.

Other Needlework

Besides sewing, there are other needlework and material crafts you can do for or with your dog. With fleece, there are cute dog-themed throws that you buy, cut to specifications, and tie—no sewing required! These are very warm and cozy, and you can easily make two—one for you and one for your dog.

Along the no-sew line, many dogs enjoy tug toys. Long strips of fake fur or fleece can be braided together and knotted at the ends to make fun tug toys. You can choose bright colors and make the size match your dog, so your Chihuahua has a tiny tug while your Mastiff has a *big* tug. Our 4-H club has made braided fleece leashes and agility slip leads by purchasing snaps or rings in bulk and then braiding around them.

Cross-stitch is very popular, and there are many neat kits that feature dogs or dog themes. You can find special embroidery and cross-stitch themes for virtually every breed of dog. After you have a pattern, you can embroider or cross-stitch clothes or items like tote bags for your dog's supplies.

Knitting has also had a resurgence in popularity in recent years. There are many patterns for dog jackets, costumes, toys, and supplies. Actually, most dogs would simply appreciate their very own afghan to lie on. Dedicated knitters may even save their dog's hair and use that to make yarn. This takes a great deal of preparatory work, but it could lead to a totally unique gift or item for you to treasure long after your dog has passed on. We have been assured that dog-hair items don't smell like dogs when they are done, due to all the cleaning of the hair. After all, your imported knit sweater doesn't smell like a dirty sheep!

Crocheting is similar to knitting, and you can make plenty of neat things—such as blankets, afghans, and toys for your dog. Before any of you boys out there dismiss knitting and crocheting, Deb went to vet school with a future astronaut who knitted a pair of socks during class, so real men do knit and crochet, too!

Latch hooking is another fun and easy needlework craft to try. This is most often done from kits that can range from simple and very inexpensive to extremely expensive. There are dog theme kits—usually puppies or cartoon characters—and wolf ones that might also appeal to you. Some of these make wall hangings, and others could be rugs or used as pillow covers.

Woodworking and PVC Construction

Woodworking can involve all sorts of things. You could stamp a design on a flat board, burn it on with your tools, and then varnish it for a beautiful wall hanging. You could also make signs such as one for your dog's crate or even one for your house.

Beyond simple woodworking like woodburning, you might want to build some things for your dog. A nice doghouse for summer shade, some jumps for agility, even big contact equipment for agility are all within the talents of a backyard carpenter. Building your own agility equipment is much cheaper than buying it.

There are plans for building agility equipment on your own, including an excellent book (see Appendix A). Much of the equipment, including jumps, is made out of PVC, so it is lightweight, easy to move, and weather resistant. Be sure to purchase PVC that is treated for ultraviolet light and maybe even indulge in some colored PVC for fun. If you become skilled at making your own equipment, you might even be able to sell some to other dog friends or barter with an agility instructor—trading jumps for lessons, for example.

If you have an artistic side, you might want to try woodcarving. Carvings ranging from simple outlines to detailed custom pieces are highly prized. You may want to start off carving soap to improve your skills and then move on to wood pieces.

Painting and Drawing

There are many fun books that teach you how to draw dogs—both realistic ones and cartoon versions. Using these can be a great place to start if you enjoy drawing or painting. You can also see whether your art teacher will let you use your dog as your model for school art projects. Kate had a project where the students had to draw an animal using pencil forms. Kate did a Corgi, and her drawing, shown in the photo on page 161, has won awards at a couple of "dog art" art shows, as well as at the county fair.

What may work best for someone whose talent is already developed is to take a photo of your dog and then do a painting or drawing from the photo. This is easier than trying to keep your dog still for a portrait! One of our 4-H members did this with her Golden Retriever, and the painting won awards at our county and state fairs. You may need to consult with an art teacher about which paints are easiest to use, clean-up tricks, and whether paper or canvas makes the better choice for your project.

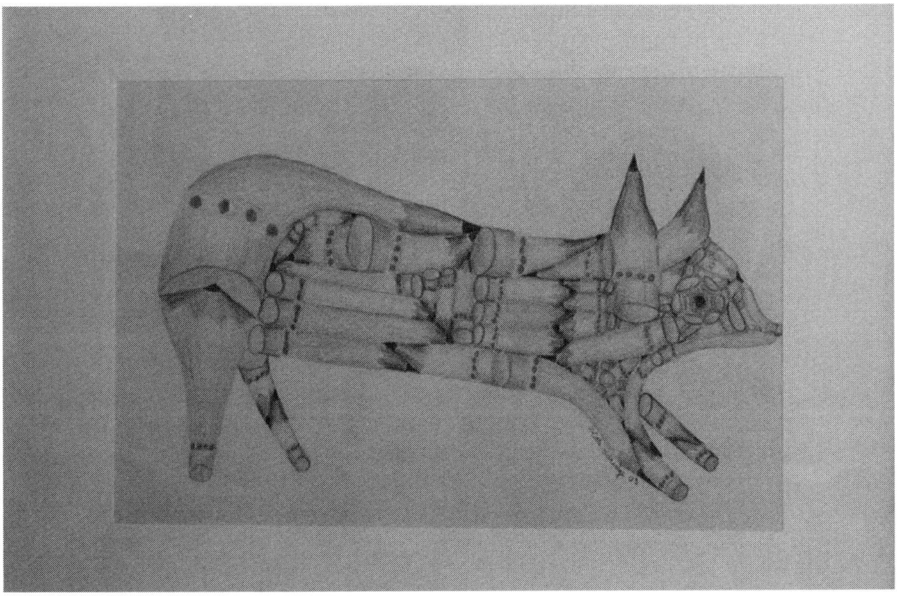

Your dog can be a model for many art projects, like this award-winning drawing.

Clay and Pottery

Clay is another great material that you can use to make gifts or other things. Most craft stores now have a wide variety of colors available, even some that glitter or glow in the dark. Most brands that you can find in a craft store can be baked in a conventional oven, which is a lot easier than hunting down a kiln to use! Even so, for big projects, this may be an easier route to take. Most communities have an arts center that has a kiln. Just track down your local kiln expert and ask him to bake your piece.

There are many different things you can do with clay. You can custom-make a food bowl for your dog; just be aware that you might need to coat it with a special varnish that will prevent your dog from getting sick. Figurines and mini statues are also fairly easy and fun to make, and with practice most people get quite good. This is where colored clay can be a lot of fun, as you can mix colors to create a dog of any color you want, be it brown and black or purple and pink! Cartoon characters often make fun models to create clay figures of.

We have also seen some gorgeous magnets and ornaments made from clay that was swirled together to create a rainbow effect, and then run through a pasta machine to make it flat and even. From there, all you have to do is cut out the shape you want! The ones we saw were cut out by hand, but for the less artistic, the imprint of a breed-specific cookie cutter will do. With this method you can also make jewelry such as pins or earrings. For magnets, you use a piece of magnet tape on the back; for pins, you glue a pin attachment on the back.

Many ceramic stores now have arrangements where you can come by, pick out a ceramic figure or dish, and then paint it yourself. The store then fires it for you so the glaze will harden, and you can pick up the finished product. Many of them have dog bowls at a reasonable price. Our 4-H group arranged for a bulk discount, and we each made a bowl for our dogs. They were beautiful and even won prizes at the county and state fairs!

Photography

Photography is certainly an art. Whether you use regular film or digital, capturing your dog in many poses and activities can be a lot of fun. Working with regular film gives you a faster reaction from the camera, and with fast film, you can capture action shots fairly easily. It still may help to set up an action shot—having your dog wait and then come through a tire jump at you, or having someone else throw the disc while you plan your shot.

Using a digital camera is nice since you can immediately see the quality of your photos and simply delete them if they are "oops" shots. It can take a great deal of experience to learn to time your shots with a digital camera, though. The reaction of the camera is slower than a regular film camera, and at first, you will find that you end up with many tail shots or even miss your dog entirely.

It can be fun to do a series of photos of your dog wearing different costumes or showing his stages through puppyhood. After all, you can't possibly have too many photos of your puppy!

Many communities have art centers that offer photography courses; also check with your local cooperative extension. To go beyond simple photos for fun, you need to do some studying (see Appendix A) and get some experienced guidance. Be prepared to accept that many shots will be rather boring until you get quite skilled.

Kitchen Delights—Doggy Style

One way to make your dog happy is to make some homemade dog treats. This is an extra-nice gift for dog friends and their people. For dogs with food allergies, homemade biscuits and treats may be the only extras they can have other than their restricted diets. Dogs who are ill or have chronic health problems may benefit from special homemade diets, too. And some families simply choose to cook for their dogs along with making their own meals. There are recipes that can be adapted for both of you!

A caution here: if you decide to cook for your dog, make sure to run your recipes or meals by your veterinarian or a veterinary nutritionist. You want to be sure your dog is getting a balanced and complete diet. Many minerals and vitamins need to be fed in certain ratios, and too much of some things can be worse than too little. Still, most dogs love your cooking, and you won't hear any fussing or complaints, even if some of your biscuits are a bit burnt on the bottom!

We have included a few basic recipes here. Check out appendixes A and C for more sources of gourmet delights.

Basic Dog Biscuits

1 cup white flour
1 cup whole-wheat flour
½ cup dry milk
½ cup wheat germ
6 tbsp shortening or bacon fat
1 egg
1 tsp brown sugar
½ cup water

Mix dry ingredients first, except sugar. Then cut in shortening until it resembles cornmeal. Beat egg and sugar together, then add water and stir in with dry mixture. Knead and then roll out to about ½-inch thickness. Cut into shapes or sizes you want. Place on greased cookie sheet. Cook in preheated oven at 325 degrees for about 35 minutes.

Dog and Cat Treats

2½ cups whole-wheat flour
½ cup powdered skim milk
1 egg, beaten
Flavoring: meat drippings, broth, or water from canned tuna
1 tsp garlic

Combine in a bowl and mix well. Dough should be stiff. Roll out to ¼-inch thickness. Cut into shapes of your choice. Bake at 350 degrees for 30 minutes.

These next few are for your dog *and* you.

Turkey Mix

1 lb ground turkey, thawed
2 eggs
Parmesan cheese to taste
garlic powder to taste

For Parents Only

This chapter is where a nondoggy parent can shine. You may not know heeling from healing, but if you can do crafts, build agility jumps, and bake dog treats, you are bound to be golden. Getting involved in doing these projects with your children will give you hours of wonderful memories along with some nice items. Granted, the floor may not get vacuumed as often (though do vacuum occasionally, if only to provide an unusual experience for your dog), but after all, what is more important—having fun with your kids or winning a Good Housekeeping award? Even Martha Stewart has dogs—OK, so she may have a number of household staff to clean, too, but still there must be dog hair around once in a while.

Craft items can be for your family's use, for gifts, or for fundraising. Our 4-H club helps pay for members to attend dog camp and other events through our fundraising as well as making charitable donations. Even great-aunt Millie might like a custom photo frame, although you may have to substitute cats for dogs as the motif.

Through doing crafts with my two kids, I have found that *I* have some new hobbies and interests—not that I wasn't already more than busy enough! Making cards for friends who need some extra cheering is fun for me and for those friends who receive them. The art of letter writing is fast disappearing, but nothing can cheer you up more than a fun card arriving in the mail. And thank-you cards from your kids are even more appreciated when they are homemade and customized. Plus, between the time spent doing these things and training and caring for your dog, your kids will *not* have any time to get into trouble!

Mix all together well. Spread out on a cookie sheet (one with sides). Bake at 350 degrees for about 30 minutes. Mix pieces in with your dog's food, or add tomato sauce and feed to your family. Works in sandwiches, too.

Cheese and Garlic Treats

1¼ cups grated Cheddar cheese
1½ cups whole-wheat flour
¼ lb corn oil margarine
garlic powder to taste
pinch of salt
milk to blend

Cream the cheese with the flour, softened margarine, garlic, and salt. Add just enough milk so it forms a ball. Chill for ½ hour in refrigerator. Roll out, cut into shapes, and bake at 375 degrees for 15 minutes or until slightly brown and firm.

Along with things to eat, there are craft projects that involve baking things such as clay or dough to create one-of-a-kind gifts. This could be a straw wreath covered with delicious homemade dog biscuits, or a similar wreath but with the biscuits varnished to stay good for many years, which makes an unusual door decoration. Just make sure that your dog isn't attracted to the wrong wreath! Many brands of clay need some heating, too. Be sure you have approval or an adult is present if the oven is to be used.

Profile: Holly and Soda Pop

Holly is a typical teenage girl in many ways. She loves to look nice, hang out with friends, eat, and enjoy social settings. Holly has a dry wit and a definite idea of what she does and doesn't like. She is also a very special young lady in that she has Down syndrome.

Holly's family is a dog family, as her parents train guide dogs. But Holly really wasn't interested in a bouncy, rowdy Labrador Retriever. She has low stamina and strength. Noisy dogs are not on the top of her favorites list, either. Still, Holly wanted to be involved with dog activities and do 4-H like her brother, Emmett.

Holly's mom did the right thing—she figured out what kind of dog would make sense for Holly and then started her research. A small, quiet, and calm dog was on the top of the list. Plus, a dog who moved slowly so Holly wouldn't have trouble keeping up. A visit to local dog shows let her mom check out many breeds and talk to contacts.

Through that visit, a contact was made with a Pekingese breeder. Soda Pop is a lovely fawn Peke who was a show dog and then retired to be a brood bitch. She had problems with her heat cycles, and her breeder wisely decided that a pet home would be the best alternative for Soda Pop. Two-year-old Soda Pop was the perfect match for 13-year-old Holly.

With Soda Pop, Holly belongs to our local 4-H group. They do obedience, rally, Junior Showmanship, and even a little agility. Soda Pop likes tunnels best! It was easy for Holly to do Junior Showmanship with Soda Pop, as she already knew breed showing. Learning to sit on command was trickier. And all of us have trouble sometimes

Holly and Soda Pop have a special relationship.

telling whether Soda Pop is sitting or lying down with her short legs and huge coat! Holly and Soda Pop like to do things together, as seen in the photo.

Holly trains and feeds Soda Pop, although her mom has to help with the grooming as Soda Pop has a full coat. Holly is also in charge of making sure Soda Pop gets her daily dose of petting and love.

Soda Pop has opened some doors for Holly. She is active in our 4-H group and is very good at crafts. She has competed at the state fair in grooming and handling and obedience. Being in 4-H gives Holly a group of kids with similar interests to interact with. She likes going to events, both to compete with Soda Pop and to help with our craft and bake sales. Being with Soda Pop encourages people to approach Holly and ask her about her dog.

Holly and Soda Pop had the top costume at our county fair. Holly wore a black dress with a white cap and white apron. Soda Pop had a harness with a broomstick attached. They were "The Maid and the Mop"!

Soda Pop is a fun little dog—beloved by our 4-H group and pretty much a mascot. She likes to play, but a rowdy Peke's idea of play is ripping up a sheet of paper towel—not charging around the house like a young Lab would. For Holly, Soda Pop is a social facilitator, best friend, and fun companion. She is the best buddy a teenage girl could ask for!

Recommended Reading

We figure that because you're holding this book, you like to read. In this appendix, we have included books and magazines that can be wonderful resources for you. Some are topic specific, and others are more general in their scope. All of them can provide many hours of enjoyable reading and inspire you to do more training and work with your dog. We highly recommend that your family read these resources together, sitting with your dog by your side.

Agility

Agility is a wide-open sport that is featured on TV when the top canine athletes compete. It can, however, be just a fun activity for you and your dog in your backyard. Don't be intimidated by the superstars you see on Animal Planet. You and your dog *can* do this, too! Check out chapter 9 for information on this sport. The following books and magazines will help you expand your knowledge of agility.

Agilityaction.com, an e-magazine for novices and anyone interested in having fun with agility.

Bonham, Margaret, *Having Fun with Agility,* Howell Book House, 2005.

Bonham, Margaret, *Introduction to Dog Agility,* Barron's, 2005.

Buckholt, Cindy, *Competing in Agility Trials—Entering Trials and What to Do When You Get There,* Clean Run Productions, 2005.

Clean Run Magazine. The first big-time agility magazine with much of the material aimed at competitors. Clean Run Productions, LLC. Contact: info@cleanrun.com.

Daniels, Julie, *Enjoying Dog Agility: From Backyard to Competition,* Doral Publishing, 1991.

Hutchins, Jim, *Do It Yourself Agility Equipment,* Clean Run Productions, 2002.

Moake, Jane Simmons, *Agility Training: The Fun Sport for All Dogs,* Howell Book House, 1992.

O'Neil, Jacqueline, *All about Agility,* Revised Edition, Howell Book House, 1999.

Boarding Kennels and Pet Sitters

Leaving your dog behind can be stressful. Chapter 12 has information to get you started, but check out the following book to help you find the perfect kennel or ideal pet sitter for your dog.

Storer, Pat, *Boarding Your Dog,* Storey Books, 2000.

Carting

Carting can be a lot of fun for you and your dog. Chapter 8 gives you the basics of the sport, and the following resources can help you along the way.

Powell, Consie, *Newfoundland Draft Work,* 1987. Order via www.nordkyn.com.

Newfound Club of America, *Draft Equipment Guide and Draft Test Rules and Regulations.* Order via www.newfdogclub.org.

Choosing a Dog

Remember that you can't choose your relatives, but you can choose your friends—and your dog can be your *best* friend. The following references help you to choose the perfect canine companion. (Also see chapter 1 to start on the right path.)

AKC, *The Complete Dog Book,* 20th Edition, Ballantine Press, 2006.

Palika, Liz, *Purebred Rescue Dog Adoption: Rewards and Realities,* Howell Book House, 2004.

Peterson, Cheryl, *Please Oh Please Can We Get a Dog? Parents' Guide to Dog Ownership,* Howell Book House, 2005.

Sternberg, Sue, *Successful Dog Adoption,* Howell Book House, 2003.

Walkowicz, Chris, *The Perfect Match: A Dog Buyer's Guide,* Howell Book House, 1996.

Clicker Training

Clicker training uses operant conditioning to help dogs learn. The following books will aid you in understanding the method and seeing whether it works for you and your dog. Warning: coordination is required! Chapter 10 gives you a quick introduction to the method, and these sources will give you more depth.

Fields-Babineau, Miriam, *Click & Easy: Clicker Training for Dogs,* Howell Book House, 2006.

Alexander, Melissa C., *Click for Joy!,* Sunshine Books, 2003.

Book, Mandy, and Cheryl S. Smith, *Quick Clicks: 40 Fast and Fun Behaviors to Train with a Clicker,* Hanalei Pets, 2001.

Delinquent Dogs

We all hope that our dogs will never be classified as juvenile delinquents, but it can happen in the best of families. Chapter 4 discusses a dog who's heading down the wrong path, and these resources give you additional options for straightening him out.

Benjamin, Carol Lea, *Dog Problems,* Howell Book House, 1989.

Benjamin, Carol Lea, *Surviving Your Dog's Adolescence: A Positive Training Program,* Howell Book House, 1993.

McConnell, Patricia, PhD, *How to Be the Leader of the Pack . . . and Have Your Dog Love You for It!,* Dog's Best Friend, Ltd., 1996.

Ryan, Terry, *Take the Lead: Leadership Education for Anyone with a Dog,* Legacy Canine and Behavior, 2002.

Volhard, Jack and Wendy Volhard, *The Canine Good Citizen: Every Dog Can Be One,* 2nd Edition, Howell Book House, 1997.

Disc Dogs

Although flying through the air after a disc may not appeal to all dogs, it can be fun even for those who stick to the ground. Chapter 9 will get you started, and the following book can help as well.

Coile, Caroline D., *Beyond Fetch: Fun, Interactive Activities for You and Your Dog,* Howell Book House, 2003.

Dog Magazines

There are magazines on virtually every dog sport as well as those with general dog information. The following are some of our favorites.

AKC Family Dog, a magazine devoted to purebred family dogs. Order via www.akc.org.

AKC Gazette, a magazine oriented to purebred dogs in shows and competitions. Order via www.akc.org.

Animal Wellness, an animal health magazine. Order via www.animalwellnessmagazine.com.

The Bark, a magazine of essays, stories, and advice. Order by calling 877-227-5639 or via www.thebark.com.

Bloodlines, a magazine for purebred dogs from the United Kennel Club. Order via www.ukcdogs.com/pubbloodlines.htm.

Dog Fancy, which is oriented to the family dog. Order via www.dogchannel.com/dog/magazines.

Dogs for Kids, a magazine devoted to dogs with kids, or vice versa. Order via www.dogchannel.com/dog/magazines.

Dogs in Canada, a publication oriented to purebred dogs and their sports from the Canadian Kennel Club. Order by calling 800-250-8040 or 416-674-3699.

Dogs in Review, which is oriented toward purebred show dogs. Order via www.dogchannel.com/dog/magazines.

Dog Watch, an educational newsletter from Cornell University. Order by calling 800-829-5574.

Dog World, which is oriented toward purebred dogs in competitions. Order via www.dogchannel.com/dog/magazines.

Front & Finish, an obedience magazine for all dogs. Order via www.frontandfinish.com.

Modern Dog, a magazine for the yuppy puppy. Order by calling 800-417-6289 or via www.moderndogmagazine.com.

Off Lead and Natural Pet, an obedience magazine for all dogs, and natural-care products information. Order via www.barkleigh.com.

Your Dog, an educational newsletter from Tufts University. Order by calling 800-829-5116.

Dogs and Kids

Obviously, this book is geared toward dogs and kids, but the following resources can give you additional insight into managing the combination of canine and child.

Kilcommons, Brian, and Sarah Wilson, *Child-Proofing Your Dog: A Complete Guide to Preparing Your Dog for the Children in Your Life,* Warner Books, 1994.

Pelar, Colleen, CPDT, *Living with Kids and Dogs . . . Without Losing Your Mind: A Parent's Guide to Controlling the Chaos,* C and R Publishing LLC, 2005.

Silvani, Pia, CPDT, and Lynn Eckhardt, *Raising Puppies & Kids Together: A Guide for Parents,* TFH, 2005.

Earthdogs

If you have a Terrier or Terrier mix who loves to dig, this is your area. We introduce earthdog activities in chapter 8, but the following book will give you in-depth information on the sport.

Murza, Jo Ann Frier, *Earthdog Ins and Outs,* OTR Publications, 1999.

Euthanasia

Unfortunately, heartbreak comes with having dogs as part of your family, as we note in chapter 6. We hope the following resources help you through some rough times.

Davis, Christine, *For Every Dog an Angel,* Lighthearted Press, 2004.

Peterson, Linda M., *Surviving the Heartbreak of Choosing Death for Your Pet,* Greentree Publications, 1997.

Sife, Wallace, PhD, *The Loss of a Pet: A Guide to Coping with the Grieving Process When a Pet Dies,* Third Edition, Howell Book House, 2005.

Flyball

Tennis balls, jumping, and running—what more fun could any dog want? We introduce you to flyball in chapter 9 and include these resources if you truly want to get involved in the sport.

Consla, Cathy, and Coleen Mrakovich *Let's Play Flyball,* Duck Ware, 2003.

Olson, Lonnie, *Flyball Racing: The Dog Sport for Everyone,* Howell Book House, 1997.

Freestyle

Music, dogs, and dancing—fun for all! This sport is covered in chapter 10, and the following book will provide you with more information.

Davis, Sandra, *Dancing with Your Dog—the Book,* Dancing Dogs Video, 1999.

Grooming

The following books can help with grooming advice.

Kohl, Sam, *All Breed Dog Grooming Guide,* Aaronco, 2002.

Stone, Ben, and Pearl Stone, *The Stone Guide to Dog Grooming for All Breeds,* Howell Book House, 1981.

Thompson, JoAnna, *In the Hands of Strangers,* Writer's Press, 2000.

Health Care

We hope, of course, that your dog will go through life healthy and happy, as we discuss in chapters 5 and 6. These resources can help you keep her that way and advise you when illness does strike.

Arden, Darlene, *The Angell Memorial Animal Hospital Book of Wellness and Preventive Care for Dogs,* McGraw-Hill, 2002.

Eldredge, Debra M., DVM, and Margaret Bonham, *Cancer and Your Pet,* Capital Books, 2005.

Eldredge, Debra M., DVM, and Kim Campbell Thornton, *The Everything Dog Health Book,* Adams Media, 2005.

Eldredge, Debra M., DVM, *Pills for Pets,* Citadel Press, 2003.

Giffin, James M., MD, and Liisa D. Carlson, DVM, *Dog Owner's Home Veterinary Handbook,* 3rd Edition, Howell Book House, 1999.

Messionier, Shawn, DVM, *Natural Health Bible for Dogs and Cats,* Prima Publishing, 2001.

Shojai, Amy D., *The First Aid Companion for Dogs & Cats,* Rodale Press, 2001.

Zink, Chris, DVM, *Dog Health and Nutrition For Dummies,* Wiley Publishing, Inc., 2001.

Herding

Herding is a wonderful team sport for you and your herding dog. We give you the basics in chapter 8, and these resources can round out your education.

Holland, Vergil, *Herding Dogs: Progressive Training,* Howell Book House, 1994.

Lithgow, Scott, *Training and Working Dogs for Quiet, Confident Control of Stock,* Queensland University Press, 1991.

Hiking and Backpacking

Let's face it—every dog can walk! Chapter 9 starts you off on a walking/hiking program, and these resources will help you to further explore the sport.

Gelbert, Doug, *The Canine Hiker's Bible,* Cruden Bay Books, 2004.

Hoffman, Gary, *Hiking with Your Dog,* Mountain Air Books, 2002.

LaBelle, Charlene, *Guide to Backpacking With Your Dog,* Alpine, 2004.

Hunting

Although most dogs today hunt for fun and to show off their instincts, there are still dogs who work for their supper. Chapter 8 gets you started on hunt training, and these books can guide you further along the path.

Bailey, Joan, *How to Help Gun Dogs Train Themselves,* Swan Valley Press, 2004.

Mulak, Steven, *Pointing Dogs Made Easy,* Country Sport Press, 1995.

Spencer, James, *Retriever Training Tests,* Alpine Publications, 1997.

Junior Showmanship

Junior showmanship is an art as much as a science. Chapter 10 explains the basics for you, and the following books help give you the finishing touches you may need to succeed.

Olejniczak, Anne, and Denise Olejniczak, *Best Junior Handler,* Doral Publishing, 1997.

Hall, Lynn, *Dog Showing for Beginners,* Howell Book House, 1994.

Haynes, Gaile, *The Winning Team—a Guidebook for Junior Showmanship,* Panache Publications, 2004.

Lure Coursing

For the speeding sighthound, lure coursing is really fun. Chapter 8 introduces you to the fun of lure coursing, and the following book will give you additional in-depth information.

Beaman, Arthur S., *Lure Coursing: Field Trailing for Sighthounds and How to Take Part,* Howell Book House, 1993.

Nutrition

If you are what you eat, you want your dog to eat the right things. Chapter 5 gives you guidelines to start with, and these resources provide additional information.

Ackerman, Lowell, DVM, *Canine Nutrition,* Alpine, 1999.

Jacobs, Jocelynn, DVM, *Performance Dog Nutrition: Optimize Performance with Nutrition,* self published, 2005.

Schultze, Kymythe, *Natural Nutrition for Dogs and Cats,* Hay House, 1998.

Obedience

A well-behaved dog is a goal for everyone. Chapters 3 and 7 help you get your dog started on the right paw. These books will help him earn his PhD.

Bauman, Diane, *Beyond Basic Dog Training,* 3rd Edition, Howell Book House, 2003.

Byron, Judy, and Adele Yunck, *Competition Obedience: A Balancing Act,* Jabby Productions, 1998.

Photography

Everybody loves to share photos of family members. Chapter 13 gives you the basics of dog photography, but for truly outstanding photos, these books are an excellent resource.

Allan, Larry, *Creative Canine Photography,* Allworth Press, 2004.

Muska, Debrah H., *Professional Techniques for Pet and Animal Photography,* Amherst Media, Inc., 2003.

Puppies

Chapters 1, 2, and 3 get you started on raising the ideal puppy as part of your family. Here are some additional resources.

Benjamin, Carol Lea, *Mother Knows Best: The Natural Way to Train Your Dog,* Howell Book House, 1985.

Hastings, Patricia, and Erin Ann Rouse, *Another Piece of the Puzzle,* Dog Folk Enterprises, 2004.

Hodgson, Sarah, *PuppyPerfect: The User-Friendly Guide to Puppy Parenting,* Howell Book House, 2005.

London, Karen, and Patricia McConnell, *Way to Go: How to Housetrain a Dog at Any Age,* Dog's Best Friend Ltd., 2003.

Rutherford, Clarice, and David Neil, *How to Raise a Puppy You Can Live With,* Alpine, 2005.

Ryan, Terry, *Puppy Primer,* People-Pet Partnership at Washington State University, 1990.

Vollmer, Peter J., *SuperPuppy: How to Raise the Best Dog You'll Ever Have!,* Super Puppy Press, 1992.

Rally

Rally, a fast-growing sport, is fun for everyone, as we mention in chapter 7. These books will give you practice courses and additional training advice.

Dearth, Janet, *The Rally Course Book—a Guide to AKC Rally Courses,* Alpine Publications, 2004.

Kramer, Charles, *Rally-O: The Style of Rally Obedience,* Fancee Publications, 2005.

Sledding, Weight-Pulling, and Skijoring

In these winter sports, running and pulling are good things! Chapter 8 gets you started with your semi-Iditarod dog, and these books will get you off to the races!

Hoe-Raitto, Mari, and Carol Kaynor, *Skijor with Your Dog,* OK Publications, 1991.

Loversen, Bella, *Mush! Beginners Manual of Sled Dog Training,* Arner Publications, 1997.

Sternberg, Mike, *Teach Your Dog to Pull,* self-published, 1988.

Therapy Dog Work

Dogs are good for you in many ways, and sharing them doubles that return. We discuss therapy dog work in chapter 11, and the following resources help you spread the love.

Delta Society, *Pet Partners Home Course Manual,* Delta Society, 2004.

Diamond Davis, Kathy, *Therapy Dogs: Training Your Dog to Reach Others,* Dogwise Publications, 2002.

Palika, Liz, *Love on a Leash,* Alpine Publications, 1996.

Tracking

The nose knows. The sport of tracking is introduced in chapter 9; these books provide you with extra guidance to help your dog use her nose to the best of her ability.

Ganz, Sandy, and Susan Boyd, *Tracking from the Ground Up,* Show-Me Publications, 1992.

Krause, Carolyn, *Try Tracking,* Dogwise Publications, 2005.

Presnall, Ed, *Mastering Variable Surface Tracking,* Dogwise Publications, 2004.

Training

The training books you might need or want can be found under the headings of "Delinquent Dogs," "Dogs and Kids," "Obedience," and "Puppies." Happy training!

Traveling with Your Dog

Dogs on the go with you are covered in these books as well as in chapter 12. You'll find out about fun deals and extra travel plans in the following books. Bon voyage!

Arden, Darlene, *Unbelievably Good Deals and Great Adventures That You Absolutely Can't Get Unless You're a Dog,* McGraw-Hill, 2004.

Fido Friendly, a travel magazine for dogs. Order via www.fidofriendly.com.

Habgood, Dawn, and Robert Habgood, *Pets on the Go,* 2nd Edition, Dawbert Press, 2004.

Tricks

Tricks are fun for everyone, and you can never have too many tricks in your dog's repertoire. So after reading chapter 10, check out some of these books for additional ideas!

Duford, Donna, *Agility Tricks for Improving Attention, Flexibility, and Confidence,* Clean Run Productions, 1999.

Hodgson, Sarah, *Dog Tricks For Dummies,* Wiley Publishing, Inc., 2000.

Palika, Liz, *The Complete Idiot's Guide to Dog Tricks,* Alpha Books, 2005.

Water Work

Water sports are covered in detail in chapter 9. These publications give you additional training advice.

Newfoundland Club of America, *Water Test Training Manual.* Order via www.newfdogclub.org.

Portuguese Water Dog Club of America, *Water Trial Manual.* Order via www.pwdca.org.

B

Organizations

This appendix contains the contact info for many organizations that are involved with dogs and dog sports. They are all excellent sources of information, and many of them have Web sites with free articles. We think they'll help you become an extremely well-informed dog owner.

Agility Organizations

These organizations offer training information and often sponsor seminars and clinics as well as national competitions. Their sites often include information on rules, equipment, and training. If they have phone numbers available, those are listed along with addresses and Web sites.

American Kennel Club (AKC)
260 Madison Ave.
New York, NY 10016
212-696-8200
www.akc.org
An organization for purebred dogs and their sports.

Australian Shepherd Club of America (ASCA)
P.O. Box 3790
Bryan, TX 77805-3790
979-778-1082
www.asca.org
This breed club allows non-Aussies in all of their performance events, including mixed breeds.

Canadian Kennel Club (CKC)
89 Skyway Ave., Suite 100
Etobicoke, Ontario M9W 6R4
800-250-8040 or 416-674-3699
www.ckc.ca
An organization for purebred dogs and their sports.

Canine Performance Events (CPE)
P.O. Box 805
South Lyon, MI 48178
www.K9cpe.com
An all-agility organization for all dogs, including mixed breeds.

North American Dog Agility Council (NADAC)
115 22 South Hwy. 3
Cataldo, ID 83810
www.nadac.com
An all-agility organization for all dogs, including mixed breeds.

Teacup Dog Agility Association (TDAA)
P.O. Box 58
Maroa, IL 61756
www.dogagility.org
An agility association geared toward small dogs.

United Kennel Club (UKC)
100 E. Kilgore Rd.
Kalamazoo, MI 49002-5584
269-343-9050
www.ukcdogs.com
An organization for purebred dogs and their sports; mixed breeds are allowed in the performance areas.

United States Dog Agility Association (USDAA)
P.O. Box 850955
Richardson, TX 75085-6955
972-487-2200
www.usdaa.com
An agility association for all dogs, including mixed breeds.

Boarding Kennels and Pet Sitters

The organizations listed here are basically professional organizations for kennel owners and pet sitters, but their Web sites do include some resources for dog owners.

American Boarding Kennel Association (ABKA)
1702 E. Pike Peaks Ave.
Colorado Springs, CO 80909
877-570-7788
www.abka.com
A professional organization for kennel owners.

National Association of Professional Pet Sitters (NAPPS)
15000 Commerce Parkway, Suite C
Mt. Laurel, NJ 08054
856-439-0324
www.petsitters.org
A professional organization for pet sitters.

Pet Sitters International (PSI)
201 E. King St.
King, NC 27021-9161
336-983-9222
www.petsit.com
A professional organization for pet sitters.

Disc Dogs

There are currently two competitive organizations for disc dog competitions. Their groups hold trials and provide some training information.

International Disc Dog Handlers' Association (IDDHA)
1610 Julius Bridge Rd.
Ball Ground , GA 30107
770-735-6200
www.iddha.com
An organization for all dogs who do disc sports, including mixed breeds.

Skyhoundz
1015C Collier Rd.
Atlanta, GA 30318
404-350-9343
www.skyhoundz.com
An organization for all dogs who do disc sports, including mixed breeds.

Earthdogs

See AKC and UKC under "Agility Organizations." All of the organizations listed in that section provide training advice and rules and regulations for their competitions.

American Working Terrier Association
15720 St. Hwy. 16
Capay, CA 95607
www.dirt-dog.com/awta
An organization for dogs that go to ground, including small Terriers and Dachshunds.

Flyball

The group listed here is the premier flyball organization. The site includes some training information.

North American Flyball Association
1400 West Devon Ave., #512
Chicago, IL 60660
800-318-6312
www.flyball.org
An organization for flyball enthusiasts; open to all dogs.

Freestyle

All three freestyle organizations in this section provide training information and support. Often, informative articles are included on their Web sites.

Canine Freestyle Federation (CFF)
14430 Overlook Ridge Lane
Beaverdam, VA 23015-1787
www.canine-freeestyle.org
A freestyle organization open to all dogs.

Musical Dog Sports Association (MDSA)
P.O. Box 141033
Austin, TX 78714-1033
www.musicaldogsport.org
A freestyle organization open to all dogs.

World Canine Freestyle Organization (WCFO)
P.O. Box 350122
Brooklyn, NY 11235-2525
www.worldcaninefreestyle.org
A freestyle organization open to all dogs and offering a junior program.

Groomers

These organizations are professional organizations for dog groomers, but their Web sites often include helpful articles for dog owners.

International Society of Canine Cosmetologists (ISCC)
18710 Kelly Blvd.
Dallas, TX 75287
www.petstylist.com
A professional organization for pet groomers.

National Dog Groomers Association of America (NDGAA)
P.O. Box 101
Clark, PA 16113
724-962-2711
www.nationaldoggroomers.com
A professional organization for dog groomers.

Health Care

These organizations are professional organizations for the most part, but they have Web sites with articles for pet owners with much valuable information.

American Animal Hospital Association (AAHA)
12515 W. Bayaud Ave.
Lakewood, CO 80228
303-986-2800
www.aahanet.org (for the organization)
www.healthypet.com (for dog owners)
A professional organization for small animal veterinary practitioners.

American Veterinary Medical Association (AVMA)
1931 N. Meacham Rd., Suite 100
Schaumburg, IL 60173
847-925-8070
www.avma.org (for the organization)
www.avma.org/care4pets (for dog owners)
A professional organization for veterinarians.

Canine Health Foundation
P.O. Box 37941
Raleigh, NC 27627-7941
888-682-9696
www.akcchf.org
A foundation via the AKC that sponsors health research to help dogs.

Morris Animal Foundation
45 Inverness Dr. E.
Englewood, CO 80112
800-243-2345
www.morrisnaimalfoundation.org
A foundation to sponsor research in animal health.

Herding

The herding organization listed here allows all herding. Look under "Agility Organizations" for the AKC, ASCA, and CKC.

American Herding Breeds Association (AHBA)
www.ahba-herding.org
An organization that allows all herding breeds and mixes thereof to compete. There are extensive articles on its Web site.

Hiking and Backpacking

Information about hiking and backpacking with your dog isn't readily available, but the following site can help.

Canine Backpacking Association (CBA)
www.caninebackpackers.org or www.caninebackpackers.com
An organization for people who enjoy hiking and camping with their dogs.

Hunting

The major clubs offer hunt tests, field trials, and competitions of various sorts. Check out the AKC and UKC under "Agility Organizations." These sites also provide educational information.

National Field Retriever Association (NFRA)
2003 N. Boomer Rd.
Stillwater, OK 74075
www.nfra.us
An organization to provide more outlets for retrievers in hunt competitions; the new kid on the block.

North American Hunting Retriever Association (NAHRA)
P.O. Box 5159
Fredericksburg, VA 22403
540-899-7620
www.nahra.org
One of the oldest hunting retriever organizations.

North American Versatile Hunting Dog Association (NAVHDA)
P.O. Box 520
Arlington Heights, IL 60006
847-253-6488
www.navhda.org
An organization that promotes using all of your hunting dog's talents.

Junior Showmanship

Junior Showmanship is done via the main breed organizations, many of which are limited to purebred dogs. The exceptions are ASCA and 4-H. Look under "Agility Organizations" for the AKC, ASCA, CKC, and UKC.

For 4-H, there are two addresses listed here: the national council and the main cooperative extension. You can look locally for your county's cooperative extension in your phone book. It may be listed under the main land grant college for your state, such as Cornell Cooperative Extension, Michigan State Cooperative Extension, and so on.

National 4-H Council
7100 Connecticut Ave.
Chevy Chase, MD 20815
301-961-2800
www.4-h.org

Cooperative State Research, Education and Extension Service
USDA
1400 Independence Ave., SW Stop 2225
Washington, DC 20250-2225
202-720-2908

Obedience

Most of the big dog organizations offer obedience training—the AKC, ASCA, CKC, and UKC are all listed under "Agility Organizations." 4-H programs also offer obedience training—see "Junior Showmanship." The following organizations offer obedience information and guidance to obedience instructors. They also certify instructors.

Association of Pet Dog Trainers (APDT)
150 Executive Center Dr.
Box 35
Greenville, SC 29615
800-738-3647
www.apdt.com
An organization for all dogs, including mixed breeds, that stresses positive techniques. They also have a rally program.

North American Dog Obedience Instructors (NADOI)
PMB 369
729 Grapevine Hwy.
Hurst, TX 76054-2085
www.nadoi.org
This organization is primarily for instructors and requires a competency exam.

Rally

There are currently three organizations that offer rally competition and information. These are the AKC (see "Agility Organizations") and APDT (see "Obedience") and the organization listed below, which is in Canada. The sites offer information on trailing and training.

Canadian Association of Rally Obedience (CARO)
www.canadianrallyo.ca
An organization to provide rally competition in Canada.

Sledding, Weight-Pulling, and Skijoring

These organizations encourage training and competing in the pulling and outdoor winter dog sports. The sites provide information on training, equipment, and competitions. Also check out the UKC under "Agility Organizations" for weight-pull competitions. Most of these organizations have junior programs.

International Federation of Sleddog Sports (IFSS)
3381 Troy Brett Trail
Duluth, MN 55803
www.sleddog.dsnsports.com
An organization for sledding and skijoring.

International Sled Dog Racing Association (ISDRA)
22702 Rebel Rd.
Merrifield, MN 56465
www.isdra.org
The best known organization for these winter dog sports.

International Weight Pull Association (IWPA)
3407 17th Ave.
Evans, CO 80620
www.iwpa.net
This group is primarily weight pulls and does have weights arranged so all dogs can pull by percentages.

North American Skijoring and Ski Pulk Association (NASSPA)
P.O. Box 240513
Anchorage, AK 99524
www.nasspa.org
This organization is based primarily in Alaska at this time.

Therapy Dog Work

All of the organizations in this section are involved in certifying dogs as therapy dogs for visitation in nursing homes, schools, and so on. These are not primarily service dog organizations, although Delta also does service dogs. Their sites include information on training, testing, and certifying therapy dogs.

Delta Society
875 124th Ave. NE, Suite 101
Bellevue, WA 98005
425-226-7357
www.deltasociety.org
An organization known for their outstanding efforts in relating people and animals.

Therapy Dogs International
88 Bartley Rd.
Flanders, NJ 07836
973-252-9800
www.tdi-dog.org
One of the oldest therapy dog groups, with a well-established certification program.

Intermountain Therapy Animal Group
P.O. Box 17201
Salt Lake City, UT 84117
801-272-3439
www.therapyanimals.org
This organization started the Read to Rover, or R.E.A.D., program for children.

Tracking

Check out the AKC, ASCA, and CKC under "Agility Organizations"; all three offer tracking programs.

Training

Check out "Agility Organizations," "Obedience," and "Rally" for sites that offer training information: the AKC, ASCA, CKC, UKC, APDT, CARO.

Water Work

Various breed clubs offer water work training and information (see Appendix A for the two most involved in water work). The organization listed here offers water work training and competitions for all dogs, including mixed breeds.

Water Education and Training Dog Obedience Group (WETDOG)
4920 Walker
The Colony, TX 75056
www.wetdog.org
An organization for water work training for all dogs.

C

Internet Resources

In our technology-based society, Web sites can be an easy way to find information you're looking for. This section contains a list of Web sites on all the topics covered in the book, from agility to obedience and beyond. Have fun surfing!

General: The Five-Star Sites

The following four Web sites belong on your list of favorites links, and they get five stars from us. We check these sites often for information and shopping opportunities. They're all easy to navigate.

www.doghobbyist.com
A site full of information and dog-related items for purchase.

www.dogpatch.org
The place for information about dog sports and activities from knowledgeable people.

www.dogwise.com
The best site for dog books you can imagine, with the latest books, oldies but goodies, and all the hard-to-find titles.

www.SitStay.com
A site our dogs bookmarked, with tons of great food, including healthy treats and unique toys.

Agility Organizations

Here are the Web sites for organizations that offer rules for competition, registration forms, and other information on the sport.

www.akc.org (American Kennel Club)
Offers agility titling competitions for purebred dogs only.

www.asca.org (Australian Shepherd Club of America)
Offers agility for all dogs, purebred and mixed.

www.ckc.ca (Canadian Kennel Club)
Offers agility for purebred dogs.

www.dogagility.org (Teacup Dog Agility Association)
An all-agility organization geared toward small dogs, purebreds, and mixes.

www.K9cpe.com (Canine Performance Events)
An all-agility organization open to all dogs.

www.nadac.com (North American Dog Agility Council)
An all-agility organization open to all dogs.

www.ukcdogs.com (United Kennel Club)
Offers agility for all dogs.

www.usdaa.com (United States Dog Agility Association)
An all-agility organization for all dogs.

Boarding Kennels and Pet Sitters

These are the Web sites of the three main pet sitter and boarding kennel organizations in the United States.

www.abka.com/abka (American Boarding Kennel Association)
A professional organization for kennel owners. The Web site also has some great resources for dog owners.

www.petsit.com (Pet Sitters International)
An online resource to help you locate licensed pet sitters in your area.

www.petsitters.org (National Association of Professional Pet Sitters)
Exactly what it sounds like: a professional organization for pet sitters! The site also includes a tool that helps you find certified pet sitters near you.

Carting

Carting is a fairly easy sport to get involved in. These Web sites are some great resources for the carting enthusiast!

www.cartingwithyourdog.com
An excellent Web site with lots of information on the sport as well as many links to other carting Web sites and sites that sell carting equipment.

www.dogworks.com
Sells carting and other equipment.

www.newfdogclub.org/WorkingDog/wdc_docs/hwd_11_draft_regs.htm
A site with the Newfoundland Club of America draft dog regulations, which give you the rules on competitive carting.

Choosing a Dog

Choosing the canine companion for you is a big decision. This Web site gives you some help.

www.canismajor.com/dog
An excellent resource for people looking into getting a dog of their own.

Clicker Training

Clicker is a fun training method, but it can be confusing! Tune in to this method with the following Web site.

www.clickersolutions.com
Covers everything to do with clickers, from getting started to training plans.

Delinquent Dogs

We hope your new dog will be the perfect companion, but just in case, here are a few Web sites that can help you out.

www.sdhumane.org
An article with some good training tips for the delinquent dog.

www.veterinarypartner.com
Advice on solving behavior issues your dog may have.

Disc Dogs

Does your dog love flying through the air after a disc? Check out these sites for information on the safest discs for your dog, as well as the rules for competition.

www.iddha.com (International Disc Dog Handlers' Association)
An organization for all dogs who do disc sports.

www.skyhoundz.com
Another disc organization open to all dogs.

Dogs and Kids

Seeing as this whole book focuses on dogs and kids, you are obviously interested in finding out more!

www.dogsforkids.com/d4k
A Web site for the magazine *Dogs for Kids*.

www.akc.org (American Kennel Club)
With a link for juniors, where you'll find information about and profiles of other kids.

Earthdogs

Earthdog is the perfect sport for Terrier breeds. Also see AKC and UKC under "Agility Organizations," as those two organizations also offer Earthdog competitions. Dig in!

www.dirt-dog.com/awta (American Working Terrier Association)
An organization that holds earthdog competitions.

www.terrierman.com/tunneltips.htm
A great Web site for getting started in earthdog.

Flyball

Flyball is fast fun with flying tennis balls and jumps!

www.flyball.org
The home site of the North American Flyball Association.

www.flyball.org.uk
A British group with plans for flyball equipment.

Freestyle

The sites in this section are for the main freestyle organizations and provide rules and training info.

www.canine-freestyle.org
Canine Freestyle Federation.

www.musicaldogsport.org
Musical Dog Sports Association.

www.worldcaninefreestyle.org
World Canine Freestyle Organization.

Grooming

The first two sites in this section are professional groomer associations; the next two give you some grooming tips as well.

www.petstylist.com
A site by the International Society of Canine cosmetologists.

www.nationaldoggroomers.com
A site run run by the National Dog Groomers Association of America.

www.canismajor.com/dog/groom1.html
Grooming tips.

www.catsanddogspa.com/page3354.html
Grooming tips.

Health Care

The first two sites here are the pet owners, areas from the AVMA and AAHA, both veterinary organizations. The next two are for foundations that support health research for dogs. All four sites provide good information.

www.avma.org/care4pets
A site from the American Veterinary Medical Association.

www.healthypet.com
A site from the American Animal Hospital Association.

www.akcchf.org
A site from the Canine Health Foundation, which is associated with the AKC.

www.morrisanimalfoundation.org
A site run by the Morris Animal Foundation.

Herding

Check under "Agility Organizations" for the sites for AKC, ASCA, and CKC, which are all organizations that offer herding. The following sites will help you, too!

members.aol.com/ccawwwsite/cca/herding.html
The site of the Working Collie Club Association with herding info useful for all breeds.

www.ahba-herding.org (American Herding Breeds Association)
Information on all breeds of herding dogs and mixes of herding breeds, too.

The two following sites are Border Collie sites but include herding information that is useful for many breeds.

www.amerbordercollie.org
A site run by the American Border Collie Association.

www.bordercollie.org
A site from the United States Border Collie Club.

Hiking and Backpacking

Checking out hiking sites for people will sometimes give you help for your dog's hiking plans as well. The sites below are specifically for people who hike with dogs.

www.caninebackpackers.com
The Canine Backpackers Association.

www.hikewithyourdog.com
Includes hiking information and guided tours.

Hunting

Check out both AKC and UKC under "Agility Organizations," as those groups sponsor a number of hunting programs. The following sites are for additional hunting organizations and provide training information, as well as rules and regulations.

www.nfra.us
National Field Retriever Association.

www.nahra.org
North American Hunting Retriever Association.

www.navhda.org
North American Versatile Hunting Dog Association.

Junior Showmanship

Check out the AKC, ASCA, CKC, and UKC sites under "Agility Organizations"—they all sponsor junior showmanship programs.

www.canismajor.com/dog/jrhandlr.html
General information on junior showmanship.

www.australianshepherds.org/juniors
This is a breed site for Aussies, but their great junior link has information that is useful for anyone.

www.4-h.org
A site that guides you to the 4-H Council for information on 4-H grooming and handling.

Lure Coursing

The following site is for a lure coursing organization. Also check out the AKC under "Agility Organizations," as they offer lure coursing as well.

www.asfa.org
American Sighthound Field Association.

Nutrition

www.canismajor.com/dog/tfood.html is a great general site with plenty of information. The rest of the sites listed in this section are associated with dog food companies, and they provide general nutrition information as well.

www.eukanuba.com
Eukanuba foods.

www.iams.com
Iams foods.

www.hillspet.com
Science Diet foods for healthy dogs.

www.prescriptiondiets.com
Science Diet foods for dogs with various health problems.

www.thehonestkitchen.com
A site on raw and natural foods.

www.waltham.com
Waltham foods.

Obedience

Be sure to check out AKC, ASCA, CKC, and UKC under "Agility Organizations," as all of those organizations offer obedience.

www.canismajor.com/dog/yobed.html
General obedience information.

The two sites below offer certification for trainers.

www.apdt.com
Association of Pet Dog Trainers.

www.nadoi.org
National Dog Obedience Instructors.

Rally

Along with the sites listed here, the AKC also offers rally trials. Check out the AKC under "Agility Organizations."

www.apdt.com/rallyo
Rally information from the Association of Pet Dog Trainers.

www.canadianrallyo.ca
Canadian Association of Rally Obedience.

www.dogwoodagility.com/store
A Web store that offers a rally e-zine that you can order.

Sledding, Weight-Pulling, and Skijoring

The first four sites listed here are for winter dog sports organizations. Also check out UKC under "Agility Organizations" for its weight-pull program.

www.isdra.org
International Sled Dog Racing Association.

www.iwpa.net
International Weight Pull Association.

www.nasspa.org
North American Skijoring and Ski Pull Association, mainly based in Alaska at this time.

www.skijor.com
A great site for skijor information.

www.skijor.org
A skijor site based in the Midwest, but with good general information.

www.skijornow.com/skijornowhome.html
A source of equipment and some general information.

www.sleddog.org/skijor/links.html
A site that provides many links to winter sports groups.

Therapy Dog Work

The organizations listed here have established therapy dog programs that are open nationally.

www.deltasociety.org
Run by the Delta Society, which also has service dog training programs.

www.tdi-dog.org
Therapy Dogs International.

www.therapyanimals.org
A site for the Intermountain Therapy Animal Group, which pioneered the Read to Rover idea.

Tracking

Tracking information can be found via AKC, ASCA, and CKC under "Agility Organizations," as they all offer tracking programs. The following below offers a wealth of tracking information.

www.geocities.com/Heartland/Valley/4425/sport.html
The site for the Moraine Tracking Club.

Training

Check out our five-star sites at the beginning of this Appendix, along with the AKC, ASCA, CKC, and UKC under "Agility Organizations," plus the obedience and rally sites.

Traveling with Your Dog

The sites listed here are directories and sources of pet-friendly places to stay, along with travel tips and guides to local activities that are pet friendly.

www.dogfriendly.com
A guide to dog-friendly travel places.

www.petsonthego.com
A site for pet-friendly travel situations.

www.petswelcome.com
A database for pet-friendly accommodations.

www.takeyourpet.com
A directory for pet-friendly places to stay.

www.traveldog.com
Travel resources for the dog on the road.

Water Work

The sites below here are resources for the dog who just can't stay out of the water.

www.dockdogs.com
Competition rules and training tips for dogs who love to leap into the water.

www.newfdogclub.org
Training tips and rules for the Newfoundland water tests (which any dog can train for, even if they can't compete).

www.pwdca.org
Training tips and rules for Portuguese Water Dog water tests (which any dog can train for, even if they can't compete).

www.wetdog.org
Water Education and Training Dog Obedience Group (WETDOG), a group that offers training tips and competitions for all dogs.

D

Hobbies and Crafts

Crafts and other hobbies are wonderful sidelines to sharing your life with a dog. Your dog may provide artistic inspiration, a willing tester for new treats, and even a model for some projects. Chapter 13 covers a number of craft and hobby ideas that can be combined with your love of dogs. We hope these lead you to many fun adventures.

Books are listed first, followed by Web sites that you might enjoy.

Cooking

Let's face it: many of us equate food with love. Cooking for your family makes you feel good and them even better. These books provide some great recipes for your dog—treats, special diets, even meals you can share.

Palika, Liz, *The Ultimate Dog Treat Cookbook,* Howell Book House, 2005.

Strombeck, Donald R., DVM, PhD, *Home-Prepared Dog and Cat Diets,* Iowa State University Press, 1999.

The following Web sites have enough recipes to keep you baking and your dog smiling for years! These are all collections of recipes for you to cook for your dog. Remember to think about any ingredients that your dog might be allergic to, and if your dog has any health problems, run the recipe by your veterinarian first.

www.azzcardfile.com/collections/dogrecipes.html
www.geocities.com/Heartland/Ranch/1011/dog.htm
www.gourmetsleuth.com/recipe_dogbiscuit.htm
www.toybreeds.com/treats.htm
www.treatworld.com

Crafts

The resources in this section include some general craft books and sites for dog items—both using dogs as models and specifically intended for dogs. You find resources on drawing, painting, or almost any craft idea not specifically covered elsewhere. Some of these books also cover multiple categories of crafts, so search away!

Ames, Lee, *Draw 50 Dogs Step by Step,* Broadway Books, 1981.

Boyd, Heidi, *Pet Crafts: 28 Great Toys, Gifts and Accessories for Your Favorite Dog or Cat,* North Light Books, 2004.

Danaher, Mary-Anne, *Pet Products for Your Dog,* Lansdowne Publishing Pty. Ltd., 1999.

Green, Gail, *The Cat and Dog Lover's Idea Book,* kp books, 2001.

Hendry, Linda, *Dog Crafts (Kids Can Do It),* Kids Can Press, 2002.

Needham, Bobbe, *Dog Crafts,* Sterling Publishing Co., 1997.

Quasha, Jennifer, *The Dog Lover's Book of Crafts,* St. Martin's Griffin, 2002.

Twitchell, Mary, *Building a Doghouse,* Storey Books, 2000.

Wellford, Lin, *Painting Pets on Rocks,* North Light Books, 2000.

Also check out the following Web sites:

www.daniellesplace.com/html/dog_crafts.html
Easy dog-themed projects for kids.

www.greyhoundmanor.com
Offers a variety of free craft directions.

Cross Stitch and Needlework

These books are wonderful resources for getting started in needlework.

Crolius, Kendall, and Anne Montgomery, *Knitting with Dog Hair,* St. Martin's Griffin, 1997.

Eaton, Jil, *Puppy Knits: 12 Quickknit Fashions for Your Best Friend,* Breckling Press, 2005.

Porter, Kristi, *Knitting for Dogs: Irresistible Patterns for Your Favorite Pup—and You!* Fireside, 2005.

Porter, Lynne, *Dogs and Puppies—the Cross Stitch Collection,* Tuttle Publishing, 1996.

Swartz, Judith L., *Dogs in Knits: 17 Projects for Our Best Friends,* Interweave Press, 2002.

The following Web sites offer wonderful canine cross stitch patterns with multiple dog breeds and dog themes featured. They also offer kits with all the necessary supplies included.

www.crosstitch.com/dogs
www.belgians.com/conbrio
www.pegasusor.com
www.twinwillowsfarm.com

Photography

See Appendix A for some great photography books.

Quilting

Quilting is becoming the new rage in craft projects. You can use the resources here to make a quilt for your dog or to make one for you.

Liby, Shirley, *Paper Pieced Cats and Dogs,* self published, 1997.

Kimes, Janet, *It's Raining Cats and Dogs,* Martingale and Co., 1999.

Malec, Sharon, *The Dog Lady Speaks,* Malec Designs, 2000.

The following Web sites offer patterns and kits, as well as pieces for your own designs.

www.doggonequilts.com
www.quiltknit.com/patterns/dogs.htm

For dog theme fabric, try the following:

www.hotdiggitydog.com
www.quiltknit.com/fabrics/dog_fabric

Rubber Stamping

Rubber stamping can make an artist out of even the least artistically talented—believe us, we know! A basic rubber stamping book will give you general guidelines; you can then indulge in great rubber stamps at our two dog stamp Web sites. Some of the stamps are works of exquisite art in themselves.

Green, Gail, *The Ultimate Rubber Stamping Technique Book,* kp books, 1999.

McGraw, Maryjo, *Creative Rubber Stamping Techniques,* North Light Books, 1998.

Ward, Nancy, *Stamping Made Easy,* Chilton Book Company, 1994.

The following two sites offer multiple breeds in their stamps and very realistic artwork.

www.catchstar.com
www.dogstampsplus.com

Sewing Projects

Check out our "Crafts" section, because many of the books listed there include sewing projects. In addition, many mainstream pattern companies, such as Simplicity and McCall's, have pet patterns.

Jenkins, Alison, *Doggy Fashion,* Barron's, 2003.

Quash, Jennifer, with Pat Hastings, *Sewdog: Easy Sew Dogwear and Custom Gear for Home and Travel,* Creative Publishing International, 2004.

Woodworking/PVC Construction

Working with wood can be fun and useful. Be sure to check out the books in Appendix A on building a dog house and building agility equipment. Remember, you may want to try any carving projects on soap first, before you move to wood. Also, follow all safety procedures when dealing with sharp carving instruments or hot tools, such as the woodburning utensils.

Kochan, Jack, *Realistic Dogs: A How-To Workbook for Carvers and Artists,* Fox Chapel Publishing, 2004.

Waters, Sue with Joanne Tobey, *Basic Wood Burning,* Schiffer Publishing, 1994.

Walters, Sue, *Pyrography Workbook: A Complete Guide to the Art of Woodburning.* Fox Chapel Publishing, 2005.

Wolfe, Tom, *Tom Wolfe Goes to the Dogs: Dog Carving,* Schiffer Publishing, 1991.

Wolfe, Tom, *Tom Wolfe's Treasury of Patterns: 90 Patterns for Dog Carvers.* Schiffer Publishing, 1998.

Also check out the following Web sites:

www.doghouseplans.com
http://futuremach.baka.com/equip.html (this site has plans for inexpensive homemade agility equipment)
www.woodburning.com/patterns

E

A Good Reminder: A Leash = Love = Life

Every day many dogs die, often painful deaths, due to the lack of a leash. That leash could be as simple as parachute cord or as fancy as custom-tooled leather. What is important is that the leash is attached to a caring owner. A dog on a leash attached to a responsible person has a much greater likelihood of a long, healthy life than a dog running free.

While your dog is on a leash, he has a greatly reduced risk of being hit by a car, being injured in a dog fight, getting lost, or being stolen. Disease risks drop, too, because you can limit your dog's contact with other dogs and with their areas of elimination. Your dog won't be in contact with wild animals. A leash can even stop a dog from picking up dangerous trash or eating rotten litter or food left around.

Leashed dogs make good neighbors and good ambassadors both for their breed and for dogdom in general. No trash raids, no eliminating on lawns, and no urinating on prized bushes. No digging up gardens or chasing cats. Joggers and bike riders are safe from pursuit. Your canine companion can't be accused of biting anyone or of siring or whelping an unintended litter.

A dog on a leash is a law-abiding citizen. Virtually all communities have some sort of leash law, ranging from restrictions for certain areas or certain times of year (most communities outlaw dogs running loose during the winter months when they might harass deer and other wildlife in the deep snow). New York has a *state*-mandated leash law, going back to a rabies epidemic, which states that a dog off his owner's property must be on leash—he cannot be "at large."

Many people move to a suburban or rural area figuring that now they can truly give Rover room to run and a chance to be free. However, it is equally, if not more, important that rural dogs be leashed or confined, just as they are in cities. Dogs seen running deer or harassing or worrying livestock can be destroyed on sight with no liability to the person defending the livestock or deer.

We would like to share with you a personal tragic story of two cute pet dogs allowed to run free. We have animals on our small farm: horses, ducks, sheep, and a pet goat, along with our house pets. To keep our animals safe, we installed a 4-foot-high, tightly woven stock fence (literally so tight and so close to the ground that the ducks can't squeeze under or through it). We did this after a neighbor's dog killed a number of our ducks last year.

Picture two cute pet dogs, about 30 to 35 pounds each (the breed is not important, because they could have been any breed or any mix). These two dogs slept in their house that night and were fed that morning from a bowl in the kitchen. They were not feral dogs, coy dogs, hungry dogs, or big and tough dogs. They were simply pet dogs someone did not quite care enough about to leash or confine; they were left to run free and enjoy the day while the family went off to work or school.

Now picture a gorgeous fall day: bright blue sky, beautiful leaves, plus a small flock of mixed-breed sheep and one lovely young dairy goat named Molly. Molly was more of a pet than many dogs—she came when her name was called, knew some tricks, and walked on hikes with us. She loved Cheerios and sliced apples. She was a beloved family member.

Deb was at the barn at around ten in the morning, and all was well. At eleven o'clock, she took her Belgian Tervuren Beep and headed to the barn to do some herding practice. She immediately knew something was wrong. The sheep were all tightly flocked together, and there was no sign of Molly. As she ran and turned the corner of the barn she saw something that will remain in her nightmares for the rest of her life.

Molly had positioned herself between the two dogs and the sheep she lived with and considered part of her family. She was fighting desperately. The two dogs were mauling her.

Deb rushed Molly to her clinic, put in an IV, and treated her for shock. Then she raced her to Cornell, where she went into the intensive care unit. Molly fought for thirty-six hours, but then the brave little goat lost her battle. The dogs were lucky: They had a quick, fairly painless death.

We had three innocent victims: a brave little goat and two dogs who deserved some training and responsible ownership. These dogs had obviously killed before. They had to be extremely determined to climb or jump that fence and then persist in attacking in the face of a 120-pound goat who was trying to fight them off. After dogs have run deer or killed livestock, they continue to do so; it is next to impossible to break that habit. If the dogs' owner had just confined them or used a leash, three wonderful animals would be alive today.

We can only hope that Molly's legacy will be that everyone who reads this passes it on and encourages puppy buyers, training-class students, people at public demonstrations, those at shelters, and all dog owners to leash or confine their dogs. The life they save could be their own dog's.

About My Dog

Name: ______________________________

Nickname(s): ______________________________

____

Breed (or Mix of Breeds): ______________________________

____

Male or Female: ______________________________

Birthday: ______________________________

Favorite Thing to Do: ______________________________

____

Favorite Toy: ______________________________

____

Favorite Place to Sleep: ______________________________

____

____

Important Information

Veterinarian's Name and Phone Number: ______________________________

____

Emergency Animal Hospital's Name and Telephone Number: ____________

____

Kennel's Name and Telephone Number: ______________________________

____

Pet Sitter's Name and Telephone Number: ____________________________

____

Type of Food: ____

____

Feeding: ____________________ (amount of food) ______ times per day

Walks/Going Outside: ____

(where / how long / how far) ______ times per day

Grooming: ____

____

____

____

Record of Vet Visits

Date: __________ Reason: ______________________________________

Date: __________ Reason: ______________________________________

Date: __________ Reason: ______________________________________

Date: __________ Reason: ______________________________________

Date: __________ Reason: ______________________________________

Date: __________ Reason: ______________________________________

Date: __________ Reason: ______________________________________

Date: __________ Reason: ______________________________________

Date: __________ Reason: ______________________________________

Date: __________ Reason: ______________________________________

Date: __________ Reason: ______________________________________

Date: __________ Reason: ______________________________________

Date: __________ Reason: ______________________________________

Date: __________ Reason: __________________

Vaccination Record

Date: __________ Vaccination: ______________________________

Date: __________ Vaccination: ______________________________

Date: __________ Vaccination: ______________________________

Date: __________ Vaccination: ______________________________

Date: __________ Vaccination: ______________________________

Date: __________ Vaccination: ______________________________

Date: __________ Vaccination: ______________________________

Date: __________ Vaccination: ______________________________

Date: __________ Vaccination: ______________________________

Date: __________ Vaccination: ______________________________

Date: __________ Vaccination: ______________________________

Date: __________ Vaccination: ______________________________

Date: __________ Vaccination: ______________________________

Date: __________ Vaccination: ____________

Date: __________ Vaccination: ____________

Date: __________ Vaccination: ____________

Date: __________ Vaccination: ____________

Medication Records

Make copies of this page so you can track your dog's medications each year.

Heartworm prevention:

- ☐ January
- ☐ February
- ☐ March
- ☐ April
- ☐ May
- ☐ June
- ☐ July
- ☐ August
- ☐ September
- ☐ October
- ☐ November
- ☐ December

Flea prevention:

- ☐ January
- ☐ February
- ☐ March
- ☐ April
- ☐ May
- ☐ June
- ☐ July
- ☐ August
- ☐ September
- ☐ October
- ☐ November
- ☐ December

Training Achievements

Check off the commands that your dog knows and will consistently obey when you ask him to.

- ☐ Sit
- ☐ Down
- ☐ Come
- ☐ Stay
- ☐ Heel
- ☐ Shake
- ☐ Roll over
- ☐ Speak
- ☐ Fetch

- ☐ Other ______________________________

- ☐ Other ______________________________

Training Goals:

____

____

____

____

____

____

____

____

____

Training Notes

Other Notes

Photo Credits

Linda Aloi: 2, 9, 88, 113, 118, 120

A-N Productions: 21

Ashby Photography: 129

Rencee Coy: 100

Deb DeVona: 94

Ricky Dutton: 33

Deb Eldredge: 16, 25, 40, 42, 65, 134, 135, 136

Tom Eldredge: 3, 13, 15, 26, 30, 39, 41, 51, 53, 57, 58, 64, 66, 69, 81, 83, 85, 97, 115, 144, 145, 152, 156, 157, 158, 161

Ingrid Friedenson: 5

Heather Gould, Watermark: 29, 62, 82, 123, 141, 142

Carl Helgerson: 104

Gerry Helmke: 106

Kathy Helmke: 76, 107

The Looris: 166

Wendi Pencille: 91

Gary Witchley: 46

Index

A

B

C

D

E

F

G

H

I

J

K

L

M

N

O

P

Q

R

S

T

U

V

W

X

Y

Z